D1388924

Native American
Cross Stitch

Native American Cross Stitch

Julie Hasler

David & Charles

A DAVID & CHARLES BOOK

First published in the UK in 1999
Text and designs Copyright © Julie Hasler 1999
Photography and layout Copyright © David & Charles 1999

Julie Hasler has asserted her right to be identified as author of this work
in accordance with the Copyright, Designs and Patents Act, 1988.

The designs in this book are copyright and must not be stitched for resale.

All rights reserved. No part of this publication may be reproduced, stored
in a retrieval system, or transmitted, in any form or by any means,
electronic or mechanical, by photocopying, recording or otherwise,
without prior permission in writing from the publisher.

A catalogue record for this book is available from the British Library.

ISBN 0 7153 0770 3

Photography by Jon Stewart
Styling by Barbara Stewart
Book design by Penny & Penny
Printed in Italy by LEGO SpA
for David & Charles
Brunel House   Newton Abbot   Devon

Contents

Introduction

Native American Indian arts and crafts are an incredibly rich source of inspiration for cross stitch designs. From beading to weaving and painting to carving, North America's indigenous folk art has so many different areas to explore. I have picked out some of the finest work by the tribes that made up the nine Native Indian cultural areas of North America, and charted it for today's cross stitchers. Where possible, I have included information about the origin of the designs and the artistic endeavours of the tribes that created them. They are not intended to be exact replicas of the originals, but my portrayal of them.

The book is divided into three sections, each of which opens with a large and vibrant portrait of a Native American Indian. These portraits will be a labour of love, a full season's stitching, but you are sure to find the finished designs of Chief Red Cloud, the Sioux warrior and the Nez Perce tribeswoman well worth the effort you have put into stitching them.

Then there are many different types of projects to bring the Native American theme into your home. The designs are beautifully presented on everything from wall hangings to cushions, and clothing to shoulder bags. Each design comes with comprehensive stitching and making-up instructions. There are also several small cards and gifts which are quick to stitch.

As in my previous books I've included a Pattern Library on pages 111 to 119. This one is a collection of fascinating borders and motifs from different tribes from all over Native America. You can either work the projects straight from the book or create your own designs by combining motifs from different charts and trying alternative colourways.

The Native American Indian theme is a gold mine for unusual designs that will appeal not only to younger stitchers, but also to anyone interested in Native American culture and beliefs, and the ways they looked at the world.

The projects opposite show the versatility of the Native American designs. Work aida and linen bands (page 113-114), rosette window hangings (page 119), a Sioux horse cushion (page 76), a Ceremonial Buffalo Skull bag (page 43), a Nez Perce bag (page 109), a Sioux Warrior pencil case (page 54), and a Sand Painting throw (page 94)

Basic Techniques

This chapter gives you all the information you need to make the projects in this book. It describes both the materials and equipment, and the stitches and techniques you'll be using, and gives hints and tips for successfully creating the designs. The final section explains how to display your finished work to its best advantage.

Materials and equipment

Needles

It is better to use a blunt tapestry needle rather than a sharp needle for cross stitch. These come in various sizes: No 24 is suitable for fabrics up to 14-count, and No 26 for 16-count and finer work.

Fabric

Evenweave fabrics such as Aida, Hardanger, Linda and Linen, on which it is easy to count the threads, are used for cross stitch. The fabrics are woven so that there are the same number of threads per inch both vertically and horizontally, allowing you to work cross stitches of equal height and width.

If you look at a piece of Aida, you will see it is woven as a series of blocks of threads: work one cross stitch over each block. Hardanger is woven as pairs of threads: work one cross stitch over two pairs of threads in each direction. Linda and Linen are woven as single threads: it is customary to work one cross stitch over two threads in each direction. Stitch one cross stitch over one thread in each direction if you want to produce really fine work.

Evenweave fabrics come in varying thread counts – in other words, you can choose the number of threads, or blocks, per inch your fabric is woven with and therefore the number of stitches per inch you will be able to sew. For example, if you embroider a design on 14-count Aida which has 14 blocks to the inch, your finished piece will have 14 stitches to the inch. However, 12-count Aida has only 12 blocks per inch, so your finished design will have 12 stitches to the inch. A design worked on 14-count Aida will be smaller than the same design worked on 12-count Aida. Linda or linen both have 28 threads to the inch, but as you usually work single cross stitches over pairs of threads, this gives 14 stitches to the inch. So a design worked on 27-count Linda will be the same size as when worked on 14-count Aida.

These fabrics are all available in a wide choice of colours, such as white, ecru, black, red, blue, green and yellow, to name but a few. The type of fabric to use is listed with each project. It you stitch straight on to a fabric which is not an evenweave, the embroidery will be distorted either horizontally or vertically.

If you want to stitch a design on a non-evenweave fabric, disposable waste canvas has made stitching designs on to all kinds of materials so simple that it is tempting to use it on everything. This special canvas, loosely woven, stiffened and held together by water-soluble glue, comes in a number of thread counts, and often contains a thread of a different colour, woven through it at regular intervals to help with counting, and to ensure the canvas aligns with the base fabric.

Try adding designs to clothing, bed linen, curtains, tie-backs, or bags using waste canvas – the list is endless. The only extra items you need are a pair of fine tweezers, and a spray-bottle of water. See the Ceremonial Buffalo Skull project on page 42 for detailed instructions.

Perforated paper is the only other stitching material used in this book. Its strength and flexibility makes it ideal for rigid items like the window hangings. This consists of a thin card which has been punched with a grid of holes the same size as

Worked entirely in whole cross stitch, the three large portraits in the book like this one of a proud Sioux warrior, are not as difficult as they may at first seem. You will probably find it easier to stitch the chart downwards, starting from the top. Check you have positioned the design correctly on the fabric by finding the centre on the chart and your fabric, and then counting up and across to where you make your first stitch. Cross off the rows as you complete them to help with counting. As you will be stitching this project over several months, try not to leave your needle in the fabric in case it leaves a mark.

14-count Aida. It can be sewn in exactly the same way as Aida, although some care must be taken not to accidentally tear the paper. Try to pull the thread gently and smoothly through the holes.

Threads

The designs in this book have been created using DMC six-stranded embroidery cottons (floss). The number of strands you use will depend on the fabric you choose to stitch on. Details are given with each project, but generally, three strands are used for 11-count fabrics, two strands for 14-, 16- and 18-count fabrics, and one strand for 22-count and finer work.

When working with stranded cotton (floss), always separate the strands and place them together again before threading your needle and beginning to stitch. Never double the thread. For example, if you need to use two strands, use two separate strands, not one doubled-up. These simple steps will allow for much better coverage of the fabric and give a neater finish.

Embroidery hoops

Embroidery hoops hold your fabric taut, which makes stitching easier, and allows the needle to be pushed through the holes without piercing the fibres of the fabric. Wooden hoops with a screw-type tension adjuster, or round plastic hoops, in the following sizes – 10cm (4in), 12.5cm (5in) or 15cm (6in) – are ideal.

Large projects such as the Sand Painting Throw, can be worked by moving an embroidery hoop around the fabric as you progress. However, you might find it easier to use a larger rectangular frame that can hold most of the fabric at a time.

Scissors

You'll need a pair of sharp embroidery scissors for cross stitch – these are essential, especially if a mistake has to be cut out – and a pair of dressmaking scissors to cut the fabric.

Relief outliner

Relief outliner, available from art shops and good craft suppliers (see suppliers list on page 127), is usually meant for glass painting. However, I used it in a number of the projects to enhance various trimmings and craft accessories. It is very easy to use – just hold the tube at an angle like a pen with the nozzle resting lightly on the surface, and squeeze gently. When you have finished, place the work somewhere warm and dust-free to dry for a couple of hours: an airing cupboard is ideal.

Preparing to work

To prevent the fabric from fraying while you are working, turn under the edges and hem, whip-stitch or machine them in place, or, alternatively, cover them with a fold of masking tape. This helps to keep the fabric neat and prevents loose fabric threads from becoming entangled with your embroidery threads.

Making a start

It is preferable to begin cross stitching at the top of the chart and to work downwards. This makes complex designs easier to follow, and allows you to cross off completed rows on the chart as you work them.

It is very important where you make your first stitch because this will determine the position of the finished design on your fabric.

First find the exact centre point of the chart by following the vertical and horizontal arrows printed on the chart with your finger to their intersection. Next, locate the centre point on your fabric by folding it in half first vertically and then horizontally, pinching along the folds. Mark along these lines with tacking (basting) stitches if you prefer. The centre stitch on your design should be made where the folds in the fabric meet.

To locate the starting point at the top, count the squares up from the centre of the chart to the top edge, then count the number of squares to the left or the right to the nearest symbol. Next, count the corresponding number of holes up and across from the centre of the fabric and begin stitching at that point. Remember that each square on the chart represents a cross stitch on the fabric.

Using a hoop

Unscrew the two rings of the hoop and place the area of fabric you are going to embroider on over the inner ring. Now carefully push the outer ring down over it, sandwiching the fabric between the two rings. Gently and evenly pull the fabric ensuring that it is drum taut in the hoop and the mesh is straight, tightening the screw adjuster as you go.

When you are stitching with your fabric in a hoop, you will find it easier to have the screw in the 'ten-o-clock' position if you are right-handed, or in the 'one-o-clock' position if you are left-handed. This will prevent your thread from becoming entangled in the screw while you are stitching.

You will probably find it necessary to tighten the screw adjuster from time to time while you are working to keep the fabric taut.

The stitches

Cross stitch

To begin the stitch, bring the needle up from the wrong side, through a hole in the fabric (as in fig. 1) at the left end of a row of stitches of the same colour.

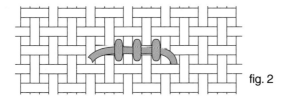

fig. 1

Fasten the thread by holding a short length of thread on the underside of the fabric and securing it with the first two or three stitches you make as in fig. 2. Never use knots to fasten your thread as this will create a bumpy surface on the back and prevent your work from lying flat when completed.

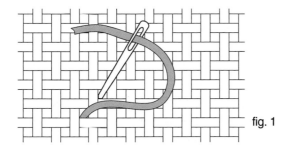

fig. 2

Next, bring the needle across one square (or block of threads) to the right and one square above on a left-to-right diagonal, and insert the needle as shown in fig. 1. Half of the stitch is now completed. Continue in this way until the end of the row is reached. Your stitches should be diagonal on the right side of the fabric and vertical on the wrong side.

fig. 3

Complete the upper half of the stitch by crossing back from right to left in a diagonal to form an 'X' as in fig. 3. Work all the stitches in the row by completing all the X's as shown in fig. 4.

fig. 4

Cross-stitch can also be worked by crossing each stitch as you come to it, for example when sewing isolated stitches on a chart. This method works just as well as the previous one, so it is a matter of personal preference. For the neatest finish, always make the top half of your cross stitches lie in the same direction. Work vertical rows of stitches as shown in fig. 5.

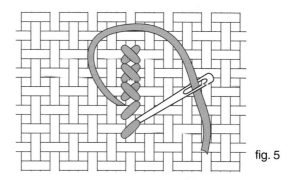

fig. 5

Finish all threads by running your needle under four or more stitches on the wrong side of the work as shown in fig. 6 before cutting the thread close.

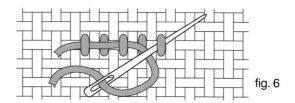

fig. 6

Basic backstitch

Basic backstitch is used in some of the designs, mainly for outlines and finer details. Always work any backstitch when your cross stitch embroidery has been completed, using one strand fewer than that used in the embroidery. For example, if three strands of stranded cotton (floss) have been used to work the cross stitch embroidery, use two strands for the backstitching. If only one strand of stranded cotton is used to work the cross stitch embroidery, one strand is also used for the backstitch.

Backstitch is worked from hole to hole in a circular backward movement, and can be stitched in diagonal, vertical or horizontal lines as in fig. 7. Take the needle down one hole back before coming up again one hole in front of the backstitch you have already worked. Do

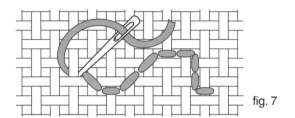

fig. 7

not pull the stitches too tight, otherwise the contrast of colour will be lost against the cross stitches. Finish off the thread in the same way as you would if you were working cross stitch.

Useful tips

1 When you are stitching, it is important not to pull the fabric out of shape. Work the stitches in two motions – straight up through a hole in the fabric and then straight down, ensuring the fabric remains taut. Make sure that you pull the thread snug, but not tight. If you use this method, you will find that the thread lies just where you want it to and does not pull your fabric out of shape.

2 If your thread becomes twisted while working, drop your needle and let it hang down freely. It will then untwist itself. Do not continue working with twisted thread because it will appear thinner and will not cover your fabric as well.

3 Never leave your needle in the design area of your work when not in use. No matter how good the needle might be, it could rust in time, and may mark your work permanently.

4 Do not carry the thread across an open area of fabric on the back. If you are working separate areas of the same colour, finish off and begin again in the right place. Loose threads – especially dark colours – will be visible from the right side of your work when the project is completed.

Finishing Techniques

Pressing

When you have completed your embroidery, it will need to be pressed so that it is flat for mounting and framing. See the cross stitch after-care instructions on page 15 if you need to wash it. To protect your work while you are pressing it, place the embroidery right side down on a soft towel and cover the back with a thin, slightly damp cloth. Press the embroidery with a hot iron. Take care not to flatten the stitches.

Mounting embroideries for framing

Before it can be framed, your embroidery will have to be stretched tightly over mounting board.

1 Cut your mounting board 2.5–4cm (1–1½in) smaller all around than your needlework fabric. Place the embroidery face down on a clean flat surface and place the mounting board centrally over it.

2 Fold one edge of the fabric over the mounting board (ensuring that it is perfectly straight) and secure it with pins along the edge of the board. Secure the opposite edge in the same way, making sure that the fabric is straight and taut on the board.

3 Use masking tape to secure the edges of the fabric to the back of the mounting board, and then remove the pins. Repeat this procedure on the two other edges.

If you find this procedure too fiddly to attempt, a company called Press-On Products Inc. has brought out a wonderful range of self-adhesive mounting boards in five different sizes. These are available from most large department stores and good craft shops. They really are a treat to work with, and make the job very easy. You simply cut the board to size as before, peel off the backing, lay your needlework fabric onto the board making sure it is centred. When you are completely satisfied with the positioning, press down very hard over the entire needlework surface. Secure the excess fabric to the back of the mounting board with masking tape.

Your embroidery picture is now ready to be framed. The best result will be achieved if you take it to a professional framer. If you are having glass in your frame, you will achieve a better effect if you use non-reflective glass. Although it is slightly more expensive it is well worth it.

Mounting embroidery in a card

Personalised greetings cards containing a small embroidery are a pleasure to make or to receive, and will be treasured long after shop-bought ones have been forgotten.

There are many types of card mounts you can buy, but the methods of assembly are the same.

Cut your fabric slightly smaller than the card mount you have chosen. Stitch your design in the centre and press it on the wrong side when it is complete. Then, iron some interfacing to the wrong side of your fabric to prevent it from fraying.

Next, centre the design in the card 'window'. Use double-sided tape to fix the design in the card window, then fold in each of the flaps in turn and secure them with double-sided tape. Check that you are folding the correct flap on to the back of the embroidery before you stick it down.

Small designs can be beautifully displayed in cards or paperweights. You will find plenty of small Native American motifs like these to choose from in the Pattern Library on pages 111–119. Shown here stitched on 22-count Hardanger in one strand of stranded cotton (floss) are the horse, bird, cactus, mountains and gila monster (the symbol for warding off evil spirits). These are charted on page 117. The cards mounts shown are DMC Studio Cards and the paperweights, which come with a special recess designed to fit embroidery, are available from Framecraft.

Transferring motifs on to card mount

To decorate cards with the Indian braves or symbolic artefacts in the Pictographs on pages 122–124, reduce or enlarge these line drawings on a photocopier to the correct size. Then trace them on to white paper or tracing paper, go over the back with a pencil, and place this paper over the card in the desired position. Go over this first with a sharp pen and then in black ink. I used a rollerball rather than felt pen because the felt-pen line might spread out over the card.

Making tassels

To make tassels to match your embroidery, cut a piece of card the length you want your tassel to be. Next, take your stranded cotton (floss) and wind it round the card from top to bottom enough times until you think it is thick enough to make a good, full tassel. I find this takes between three-quarters and a whole skein.

Thread your needle with a length of matching stranded cotton (floss), and push it under the wound thread at one end of the card. Tie the two ends securely, but do not trim them. Using a sharp pair of scissors, snip through the wound thread at the opposite end as in fig. 8, and remove the card. Wind more matching stranded cotton (floss) around the bundle about 1cm (⅜in) away from the tied end. Tie securely, and hide the loose ends in the bundle of wound threads.

Trim the loose tassel ends to neaten and straighten if necessary, and brush out with a firm, fine brush to

separate the strands of thread. Attach the tassel to your embroidery by threading your needle with the two ends you left hanging earlier, and sewing it to your fabric.

If you wish to add pony beads to your tassel, you should thread them on to the tied end before sewing the tassel to your embroidery fabric.

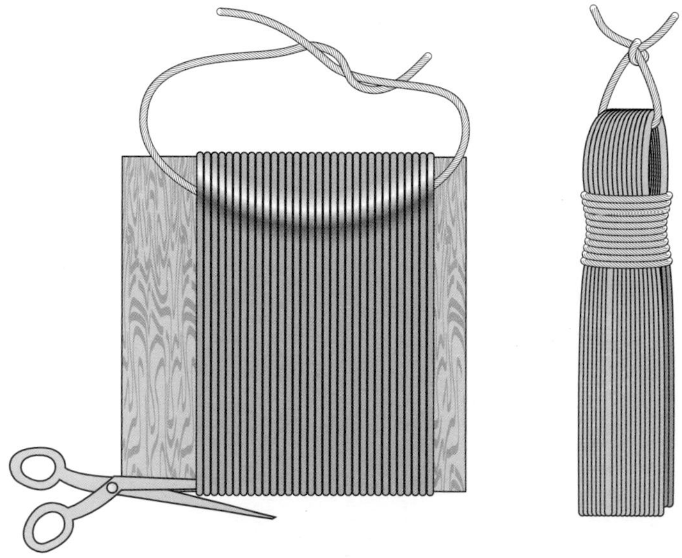

Securing beads to laces

Secure pony beads to a deerskin lace tail by tying a knot at the tail end. Or, place a drop of craft adhesive below the last bead on the tail, and slide the bead over the glue. Set aside and leave to dry. Use the same procedure for the metal cones.

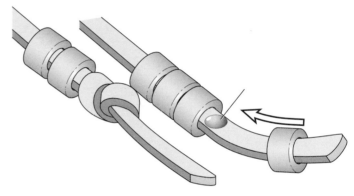

fig. 9 Securing pony beads to a deerskin lace tail

Securing feathers to laces

To secure the feathers and fluffs on the lace tails, first thread the pony beads on to the lace. Lay the feather quill over the lace below the last bead, and glue into place with craft adhesive. Slide the bead over the feather quill to hold in place as in fig. 10. Use this method for securing other craft accessories too.

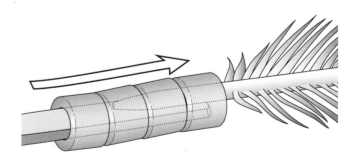

fig. 10 Securing feathers to lace tails

fig. 8 Making tassels for your embroidery

Simple repeating motifs are ideal for stitching on aida and linen bands.
You will find the chart for the designs shown here on page 113–114

Cross stitch after-care

You may find at some stage, that your cross stitch projects need to be laundered. This is no problem: follow the simple advice recommended by DMC in conjunction with their stranded cotton (floss).

Washing
Cotton or linen fabric
Wash separately from all other laundry, by hand in warm soapy, water. Rinse thoroughly. Squeeze without twisting and hang out to dry. Iron on the reverse side using two layers of white linen.

Synthetic fabric
Not recommended

Bleaching or whitening agent
Cotton or linen fabric
Dilute product according to manufacturer's instructions.

Pre-soak the embroidery in clear water, then soak for 5 minutes in a solution of about one tablespoon of disinfectant per litre (2pt) of cold water. Rinse thoroughly in cold water.

Synthetic fabric
If the white of the fabric is not of a high quality, follow the above instructions. If it is a pure white (white with a bluish tinge) do not use bleaching or whitening agent.

Dry cleaning
Cotton or linen fabric
Avoid dry cleaning. Some spot removers (benzine, trichloroethylene) can be used for small stains.

Synthetic fabric
NOT RECOMMENDED, even for a small stain.

The Spirit World

Native American Indians saw the world as the theatre of spirit beings. They believed that the sky, the earth, and all the plants, birds and animals in it had spirits that must be respected. To them, there was no clear division between human beings and the spirit world.

These spirits were reached through dance, song, and prayer, when the spirits would take possession of them. The tribes would offer gifts to the spirits, including fasting and sacrifices or offerings. In return, the spirits would bring gifts to the people. The greatest of these were favourable weather conditions, good crops or hunting, and the thriving of the culture itself. Many tribes also believed in ancestral spirits which looked after each family, passing on information through dreams.

The designs in this section reflect the importance of the spirit world in the lives of Native American tribes. A buffalo skull, a peace pipe, a bear claw amulet, a shaman's medicine bag, as well as a Dream Catcher wall hanging are among the ceremonial objects portrayed in cross stitch. But first, there's a portrait of the great Sioux chief Red Cloud, who fought to uphold the traditions of his people.

The first of the three magnificent large portraits in the book shows the proud and fearless Sioux chief Red Cloud, who fought to preserve his people's way of life and hunting grounds.

Chief Red Cloud

According to Native American legend, a meteor flamed in the skies the year Red Cloud (1822-1909), leader of the Oglala Sioux, was born. When the white man built roads and forts on their best hunting lands, the Oglala Sioux went to war, led by Chief Red Cloud. They attacked forts and waggon trains until finally the Government in Washington withdrew. Red Cloud signed a treaty of peace, agreeing to end all war forever.

The Government agreed to a Sioux Reservation comprising half of South Dakota and a vast 'unceded Indian territory' in Wyoming and Montana 'as long as the grass shall grow'.

'Red Cloud's War' was the only conflict won by the American Indians against the Government and it earned the chief deep respect from his people. Red Cloud kept his word to live in peace yet at the same time he always strived to preserve the traditions of the Oglala Sioux.

The Lakota Sioux lived in the Plains region. They were such a large tribe, that they divided up into seven separate bands, the most powerful one being the Oglala.

The portrait

You can either stitch the whole portrait of the famous Sioux chief, or use the border from this design to make a beautiful mirror frame.

- ✡ White Aida fabric, 14-count, 71 x 55cm (28 x 21¾in)
- ✡ DMC stranded cotton (floss) in the colours listed on the chart
- ✡ Tapestry needle, No 24
- ✡ Firm mounting board, 63.5 x 47.5cm (25 x 18¾in)
- ✡ Masking tape
- ✡ Picture frame of your choice

1 Prepare your fabric, find the starting point (see page 10) then, following the Chief Red Cloud chart on pages 20 to 23, work the design downwards. Use two strands of stranded cotton (floss) throughout.

2 When you have completed the embroidery, place it face down on a soft cloth or towel and press it carefully (see page 12).

3 See 'Mounting embroideries for framing' on page 12 to mount and frame the finished embroidery.

The mirror

The original border to the Chief Red Cloud chart on pages 20–23 features eight pattern repeats on each side, but I included only six here to make the mirror more of a square, and adjusted the colour of the repeats accordingly.

- ✡ White Hardanger fabric, 22-count, 41 x 37cm (16⅛ x 14⅝in)
- ✡ DMC stranded cotton (floss) in the colours listed on the chart
- ✡ Tapestry needle, No 26
- ✡ Mounting board, 33.2 x 29.5cm (13⅛ x 11⅝in)
- ✡ Mirror cut to the same size as the mounting board
- ✡ Masking tape
- ✡ Scalpel or craft knife
- ✡ Double-sided adhesive tape
- ✡ Picture frame of your choice

1 Prepare your fabric, find the starting point (see page 10) then, following the border design from the chart on pages 20-23, work the design downwards. Use one strand of stranded cotton (floss) throughout.

2 When you have completed the embroidery, press, following the instructions on page 12.

3 From the mounting board, carefully cut out a central window measuring 13.2 x 11.3cm (5¼ x 4½in). Place

your embroidery face down on a firm, flat surface and position the mounting board on top of it ensuring it is positioned accurately.

4 Next, mark the cut-out on the fabric with a soft pencil. Using a sharp pair of scissors, make a small nick in the centre of the fabric, and cut diagonally from the centre out to each marked corner. Place the mounting board over the fabric again, and fold the triangles of

fabric to the back of the board, securing them with masking tape. Next, fold in the outer edges of fabric, mitring the corners and securing them with tape.

5 Fix your mirror into position with the double-sided tape. See 'Mounting embroideries for framing' on page 12 to mount and frame your finished embroidery.

The repeating border pattern can be used to decorate a mirror frame.

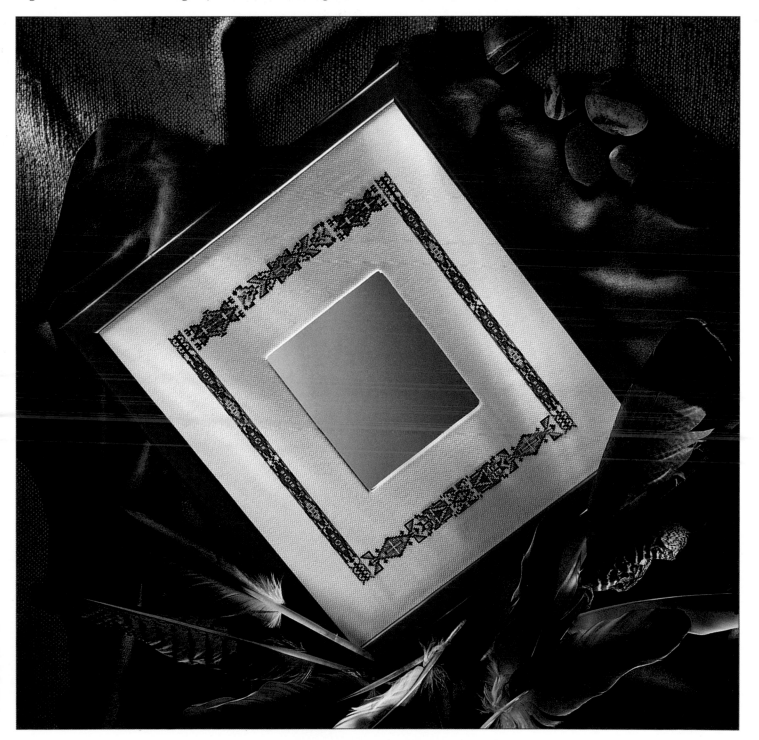

Chief Red Cloud
DMC Stranded Cotton (Floss)

⊡	Blanc	⊠	822
⊠	300	●	823
⊿	301	⊡	824
◨	304	◨	827
◼	310	◺	839
⊡	317	⊟	840
↑	318	◹	841
▥	321	‖	842
◪	349	◪	869
⊞	413	◆	898
○	414	▮	904
▷	415	◇	921
◹	420	◪	924
✦	434	◀	938
∩	451	<	950
←	471	∧	972
⋀	502	⅃	973
⊥	535	▤	975
▦	600	→	977
▨	632	S	995
▨	666	∨	996
⊡	676	▲	3031
⊘	720	↓	3064
÷	746	⋈	3346
◣	796	▶	3371
⅂	797	+	3706
+	800	▽	3772
⊤	801	⊙	3799
◼	814	▨	3801
◪	815	U	3826
▨	816	⊤	3829

Chief Red Cloud

DMC STRANDED
COTTON (FLOSS)

⊡	Blanc	▨	822
▣	300	●	823
▨	301	▣	824
◪	304	▥	827
▪	310	↘	839
▢	317	—	840
↑	318	◺	841
▛	321	▥	842
◣	349	◩	869
▥	413	◈	898
○	414	▮	904
⊳	415	◇	921
◺	420	▪	924
◪	434	◀	938
⌒	451	◁	950
←	471	∧	972
∧	502	⌇	973
▮	535	▐	975
▤	600	→	977
◤	632	▤	995
▨	666	∨	996
⅃	676	▲	3031
⊘	720	↓	3064
⊡	746	✕	3346
▼	796	▶	3371
◥	797	+	3706
⊹	800	▽	3772
▜	801	◉	3799
▎	814	◪	3801
◱	815	⋃	3826
◪	816	◫	3829

Ceremonial Dance

Ceremonial dances were at the heart of Native American Indian culture. Through them the tribes expressed their hopes and fears in a highly symbolic way. Most of the dances had a definite purpose: offering prayers for rain, the success of the hunt, or a flourishing harvest, for example. In others, such as the Eagle dance and the Buffalo Dance, the braves impersonated animals by putting on symbolic head-dresses or costumes to implore the forces of nature. War dances were held to incite the warriors before they went into battle, and victory dances celebrated their return. There were also dances for healing, for death and marriage, and others simply for pleasure. Most were colourful and dramatic events.

I found the best way to capture the grace and exciting movements of these ceremonial dancers was to draw the figures as a single block of colour.

Framed picture

You can either stitch all four figures within a striking border to make a framed picture or stitch them individually to go in cards.

✡ White Aida fabric, 14-count, 45 x 61cm (17¾ x 24in)
✡ DMC stranded cotton (floss) in the colours listed on the chart
✡ Tapestry needle, No 24
✡ Firm mounting board, 37.5 x 53cm (14¾ x 21in)
✡ Masking tape
✡ Picture frame of your choice

1 Prepare your fabric, find the starting point (see page 10) then, following the Ceremonial Dance chart on pages 26 and 27, work the design downwards. Use two strands of stranded cotton (floss) throughout.

2 When you have completed the embroidery, place it face down on a soft cloth or towel and press it carefully (see page 12).

3 See 'Mounting embroideries for framing' on page 12 to mount and frame the finished embroidery.

Greetings cards

Each of the figures looks good mounted on its own in a card decorated with a Concho or a Critter spot.

For each card you will need:

✡ Sky blue Aida fabric, 18-count, 17.5 x 13.5cm (7 x 5¼in)
✡ DMC stranded cotton (floss) in the colours listed on the chart
✡ Tapestry needle, No 26
✡ Large Crafta Card, 20 x 15cm (7⅞ x 5⅞in) with a 139 x 95mm (5½ x 3¾in) rectangular aperture, available from Framecraft Miniatures (see suppliers list on page 127)
✡ Medium-weight iron-on interfacing (optional)
✡ Double-sided adhesive tape
✡ Concho or Critter spot of your choice, available from Pearce Tandy Leathercraft (see suppliers list on page 127)
✡ Jewellery pliers
✡ Scalpel or craft knife

1 Prepare your fabric, find the starting point (see page 10) then, following the chosen figure from the chart on pages 26 and 27, work the design downwards. Use two strands of stranded cotton (floss) throughout.

2 When you have completed the embroidery, place it face down on a soft cloth or towel and press it carefully (see page 12). Iron the interfacing to the wrong side. See page 13 for mounting embroidery in a card.

3 Place your card face up on a firm, flat surface, take your chosen spot, decide where you want to position it on the card, and press it firmly onto the card mount, so that the back prongs make an impression in the card. With the scalpel or craft knife, make a small cut all the way through the card mount where the impressions are.

4 Push the back prongs of the spot through these cuts, and fasten by bending the prongs over using the jewellery pliers.

Bookmark

You can also take a section of the decorative border as your chart, to make a distinctive bookmark decorated with a pony bead tassel. Turn to page 121 for the photograph of this project.

✡ White Aida fabric, 14-count, 26.5 x 9.5cm (10½ x 3¾in)
✡ Medium-weight iron-on interfacing, 26.5 x 9.5cm (10½ x 3¾in)
✡ DMC stranded cotton (floss) in the colours listed on the chart
✡ Tapestry needle No 24
✡ Matching sewing thread
✡ Tassel in a colour to match the stranded cotton (floss)
✡ Pony bead

1 Prepare your fabric, find the starting point (see page 12) then, following the border design from the chart on pages 26 and 27, work the design downwards. Use two strands of stranded cotton (floss) throughout.

2 When you have completed the embroidery, place it face down on a soft cloth or towel and press it carefully (see page 12). Iron the interfacing to the wrong side of the embroidery.

3 Place the embroidery right side up on a firm, flat surface, and fold in half lengthwise. Pin, tack and stitch a 1cm (⅜in) seam down this long edge. Trim the seam and press it open, ensuring that the embroidery is central on the front.

4 Stitch the bottom edge to a point 2.5cm (1in) below the embroidered motif, and clip any excess fabric. Turn to the right side.

5 Press in the seam allowance on the top edges, and slip stitch together to close. Thread the pony bead on to the tassel (see page 14), and hand stitch the tassel to the point on the bottom edge.

Ceremonial Dance

DMC Stranded
Cotton (Floss)

- ● 310
- ▨ 606
- ◪ 973
- ⊠ 996
- Backstitch
- ◪ 310

Dream Catcher, Sun Catcher, Medicine Wheel

The Dream Catcher appears in many Native American cultures. If you can catch your bad dreams, it was thought, you will be blessed with happy sleep, so it was common practice to hang a symbolic object decorated with feathers, made from willow branches and sinew, above the bed at night. The tribes also made Sun Catchers to celebrate the sun's vital role in their lives which they decorated with bright colours and sparkling beads to remind them of the beauty of a summer's day. The Medicine Wheel, another sacred object, symbolised balance, harmony and brotherhood and served as a reminder of the Native American belief, that "We are all related – to everyone and to everything".

According to legend, the original Dream Catcher was given to man by a spider, a willow tree, and an eagle. The spider told man to hang it over his bed where all dreams from the spirit world have to pass. The spider bent the branches of the willow into a circle connecting all the people of the world. She spun her web of wisdom around the willow branches to catch the people's bad dreams and hold them until the rays of the morning sun turned them into dew. These dreams trickled down the length of the eagle feather and were given to the earth. Good dreams circle the hoop and filter through the web, blessing the sleeper with happy sleep.

Dream Catcher

Make your own Dream Catcher suspended between two stout sticks to hang in your home, and decorate it with feathers and Critter Spots.

✡ Sky blue Aida fabric, 14-count, 69 x 33cm (27¼ x 13in)
✡ Contrasting backing fabric, 14-count, 69 x 33cm (27¼ x 13in)
✡ DMC stranded cotton (floss) in the colours listed on the chart
✡ Tapestry needle, No 24
✡ Matching sewing thread
✡ Two deerskin laces, 64cm (25in) long
✡ A selection of feathers, bells, charms, Critter Spots, etc. to hang from the laces
✡ Pony beads in colours of your choice
✡ Two 2.5cm (1in) wooden poles or sticks, 45.5cm (18in) long
✡ All measurements include a 13mm (½in) seam allowance

1 Prepare your fabric, find the starting point (see page 10) then, following the Dream Catcher chart on pages 32 to 34, work the design downwards. Use two strands of stranded cotton (floss) for the cross stitch, and one strand for the backstitch.

2 When you have completed the embroidery, place it face down on a soft cloth or towel and press it carefully (see page 12).

3 Place the embroidered fabric face up on a firm, flat surface with the lining on top, right sides facing. Pin and tack (baste) together along all edges, leaving a 12.5cm (5in) opening on one short edge for turning.

4 Machine stitch the fabrics together. Remove the pins and tacking (basting) stitches.

5 Press the seams open, trim any excess fabric from the corners, turn to the right side and press. Turn in the seam allowance on the opening, and slip stitch to close. Turn over a 5cm (2in) hem at the top and bottom edges and slip stitch in place, making casements for the poles or sticks to go through.

6 Tie the deerskin lace into place around the wooden pole or stick at the top, leaving a loop for hanging the embroidery and enough at the ends for decorating. Add more laces to the poles or sticks, tying them in place as desired. Thread the pony beads onto the ends of the laces and add the feathers or charms, fixing them as described on page 14. I used Guinea Hen Fluffs and White Fluffy Plumes, Turtle Critter Spots, and 2.3cm (⅞in) nickel-plated dance bells.

Sun worship was important to the Native Americans. Tribes of the South-eastern and South-western regions depended on the sun for their crops. Most Plains tribes performed annual sun dances which they believed would keep away famine and enemies. Tribes of Alaska and other northern areas, longed for the light and warmth of the sun during the long dark winters.

Sun Catcher

The Native Americans loved bright colours and the effect of light on glass beads, and they incorporated both of these in their Sun Catchers. Why not make several Sun Catchers to hang in your windows and capture the rays of the sun?

- Mill Hill silver perforated needlework paper, 14-count, one 23 x 30.5cm (9 x 12in) sheet
- Heavy-weight iron-on interfacing, slightly smaller than the perforated paper
- DMC stranded cotton (floss) in the colours listed on the chart
- DMC fil argent mi-fin silver thread
- Tapestry needle, No 24
- Craft adhesive
- Masking tape
- Scalpel or craft knife
- Small watercolour paintbrush
- Tube of silver relief outliner
- One deerskin lace
- DMC glass needlecraft beads in colours of your choice
- Various items to hang from the design, such as bells, feathers, chimes, beads or charms. I used silver fetish charms.

1 Find the starting point on the perforated paper (see page 10, find the centre by drawing a vertical and a horizontal line in pencil rather than folding the paper). Following the chart on page 35, work the design downwards. Use two strands of stranded cotton (floss) throughout. Remember to handle the perforated paper with care, and try not to bend it while stitching.

2 When you have completed the embroidery, place it face down on a soft cloth or towel and iron the interfacing on to the wrong side of the work to give it added strength.

3 Place the work face up on a firm, flat surface, and outline the design with the relief outliner, as detailed on page 10. Leave to dry.

4 Cut out the design with the scalpel or craft knife, cutting as close as possible to the outline. Squeeze a little of the relief outliner into a small container, and brush around the edges of the design to cover up the raw edges with the paintbrush.

5 Decide on the position, length and number of beads and charms to go on each bead hanging. To make each one, cut approximately 50.5cm (20in) of fil argent mi-fin silver thread. Thread it with glass beads in your chosen colour to make the bottom loop (I used 19). Then double it up in the needle and continue to thread on your chosen beads and charms, until you are happy with the way it looks.

6 When you have done this for each length, and cut a piece of deerskin lace for the central hanging loop at the top, turn the work over so that the wrong side is facing you, and position each length in the desired place, ensuring the top bead just touches the silver outline. Temporarily fix the loose ends of thread to the interfacing with a piece of masking tape.

7 Using the watercolour brush, brush craft adhesive over the silver thread ends for approximately 2.5cm (1in), removing the masking tape and trimming off excess thread when the adhesive is thoroughly dry. Mark the top centre point, and fix the deerskin lacing into place for the hanging loop using the craft adhesive.

Medicine Wheel

Make a traditional Medicine Wheel and decorate it with pony beads and feathers to hang in your home.

- Mill Hill ecru perforated needlework paper, 14-count, one 23 x 30.5cm (9 x 12in) sheet
- Heavy-weight iron-on interfacing (as for Sun Catcher)
- DMC stranded cotton (floss) in the colours listed on the chart
- Tapestry needle, No 24
- Craft adhesive
- Scalpel or craft knife
- Black relief outliner
- One deerskin lace
- Pony beads
- Three feathers
- Yellow acrylic paint

1 Work the design following the stitching instructions given for the Sun Catcher. Decide on the number of pony beads and the type of feathers to include (I used White Fluffy Plumes and a Red-topped Pheasant

Feather). This will determine the length of each lace. Cut four pieces of deerskin lace to the required length, (remember to make the piece for the hanging loop twice as long because it will be doubled up) and paint the right side with yellow acrylic paint.

2 Thread the beads on to each lace (remembering to double up the lace for the hanging loop), and fix the feathers to the laces (see 'Securing feathers to laces' on page 14). When you have done this, turn the work over so that the wrong side is facing you, and fix each lace into place in line with the centre cross on the design, using the craft adhesive.

Representing the wheel of life, the cross in the centre of the Medicine Wheel symbolises the four winds, four seasons, four directions and four corners of the earth. The colours at each corner represent the four colours of people – Red, Yellow, Black and White.

The flexibility and strength of perforated paper make it the perfect medium for a stitched window hanging. Stitch your own Sun Catcher and Medicine Wheel window hangings and decorate them with glass beads, silver fetish charms, pony beads, feathers or even gem stones traditionally associated with Native American Indian culture.

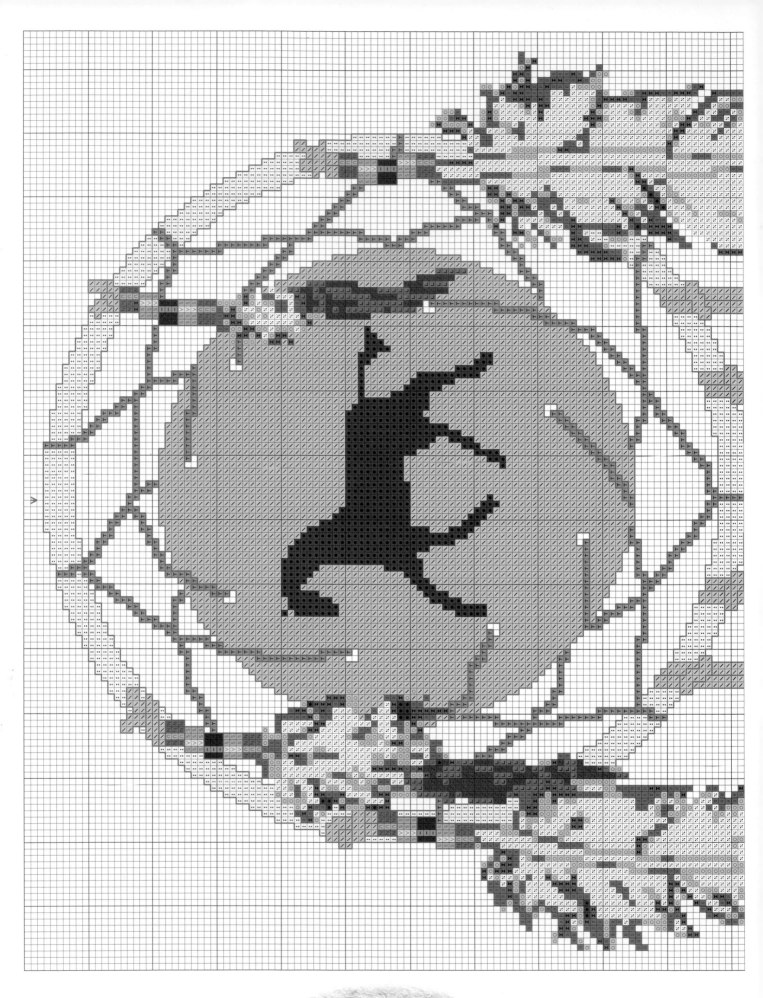

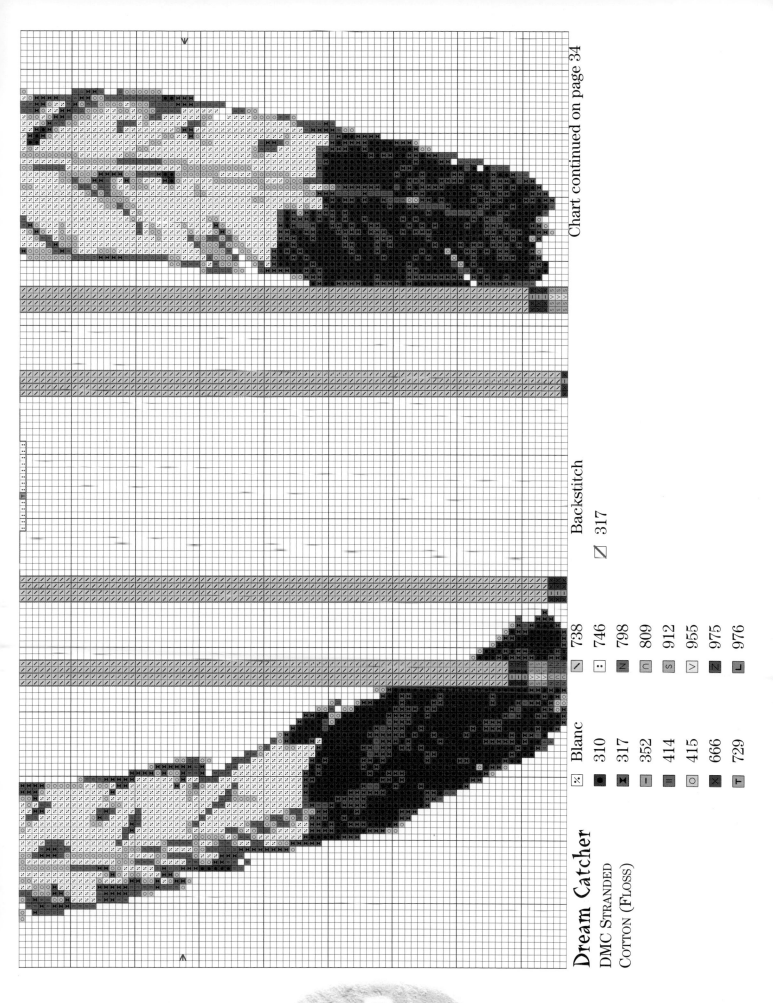

Dream Catcher

DMC Stranded Cotton (Floss)

⁒ Blanc	/ 738			
● 310	∷ 746			
✕ 317	N 798			
I 352	∩ 809			
= 414	s 912			
○ 415	V 955			
✕ 666	Z 975			
T 729	L 976			

Backstitch

∕ 317

Chart continued on page 34

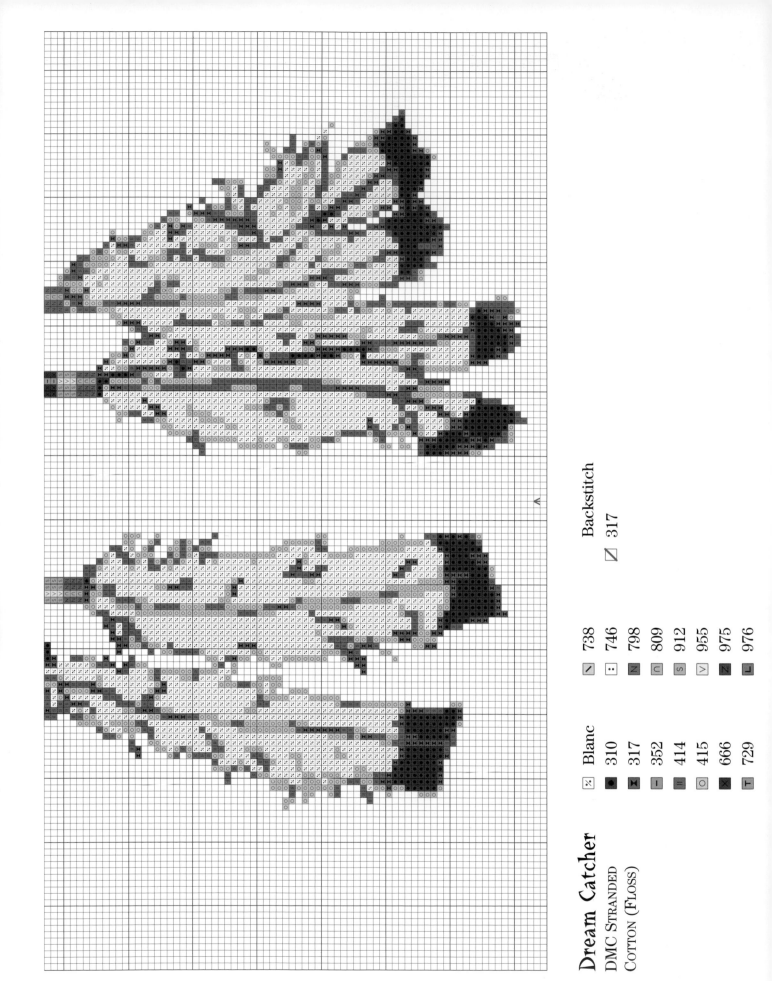

Dream Catcher

DMC Stranded
Cotton (Floss)

	Blanc		738
●	310	∴	746
✕	317	И	798
I	352	∪	809
=	414	S	912
○	415	V	955
✕	666	Z	975
T	729	L	976

Backstitch

∕ 317

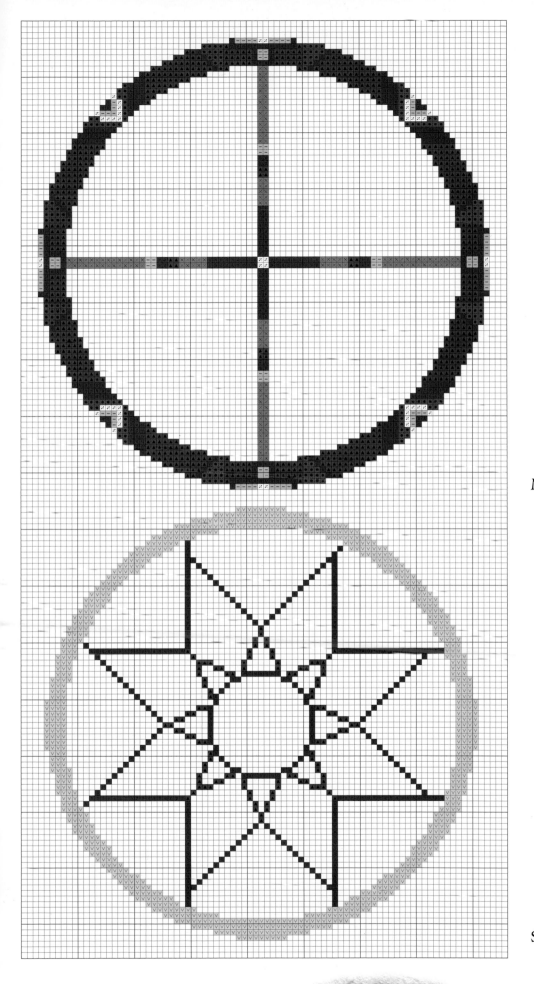

Sun Catcher and Medicine Wheel

DMC STRANDED
COTTON (FLOSS)

⊠ Blanc
● 310
▐ 606
✕ 782
▲ 797
– 996
∨ 3821

Medicine Wheel

Sun Catcher

Plains Warrior

A Native American Indian man gained honour through bravery in war, and boys longed to become members of a warrior society. Each society had its own costumes, songs and dances, and organised raids against its enemies. The greatest act of bravery during battle was to touch the enemy with bare hands or a long stick known as a coup stick. A tally was kept of all such coups or blows and it was considered shameful to have a coup count against you. A warrior would proudly display his coups for all to see, either by adding feathers to his war bonnet or war shirt, or by cutting notches on his coup stick. Now you can stitch a proud Plains warrior as he returns from battle.

The wall hanging

Stitch the Plains warrior chart on a sky blue fabric background and make it into a wall hanging decorated with Native American beads and arrowheads.

- ✡ Sky blue Aida fabric, 18-count, 45 x 27cm (17¾ x 10¾in)
- ✡ Contrasting backing fabric, 45 x 27cm (17¾ x 10¾in)
- ✡ DMC stranded cotton (floss) in the colours listed on the chart
- ✡ Tapestry needle, No 26
- ✡ Matching sewing thread
- ✡ One 3cm (1¼in) Santa Fe Concho
- ✡ Thirty-six pony beads
- ✡ Four 2.5cm (1in) bone hair pipes

- ✡ Four 2cm (¾in) metal arrowheads
- ✡ Two deerskin laces, 64cm (25in)
- ✡ Twelve small feathers or fluffs
- ✡ Craft adhesive
- ✡ Small watercolour brush
- ✡ Two 13mm (½in) wooden poles or sticks, 35.5cm (14in) long

All measurements include a 13mm (½in) seam allowance

1 Prepare your fabric, find the starting point (see page 10) then, following the Plains Warrior chart on pages 38 to 39, work the design downwards. Use two strands of stranded cotton (floss) throughout.

2 When you have completed the embroidery, place it face down on a soft cloth or towel and press it carefully (see page 12).

3 Place the embroidered fabric face up on a firm, flat surface with the lining fabric on top, right sides facing. Pin and tack (baste) together along all edges, leaving a 10cm (4in) opening on one short edge for turning. Machine stitch the fabrics together. Remove pins and tacking (basting) stitches.

4 Press the seams open, trim any excess fabric from the corners, turn to the right side and press. Turn in the seam allowance on the opening, and slip stitch together. Turn over a 5cm (2in) hem at the top and bottom edges and slip stitch in place, making casements for the poles or sticks to go through.

5 Tie the deerskin lace into place around the top of the wooden pole or stick, leaving a loop for hanging and enough at the ends for decorating. Add more laces to the bottom pole, tying them in place as desired. Decorate with the pony beads and feathers (I used Heart Pheasant Fluffs), fixing them as described on page 14.

6 To make the concho decoration, take your concho, thread the laces through the slits in the middle and tie in place. Position this centrally on the unstitched fabric below the design. Using the watercolour brush, apply a small amount of craft adhesive around the edge of the concho on the wrong side, and press it firmly onto the work. Set aside and leave to dry.

7 Thread the pony beads onto each of the concho lace ends, split the ends of the lace in half for 4.5cm (1¾in) and add a 2.5cm (1in) bone hair pipe to each split end. Finish off each end with a 2cm (¾in) metal arrowhead, fixing them as described on page 14.

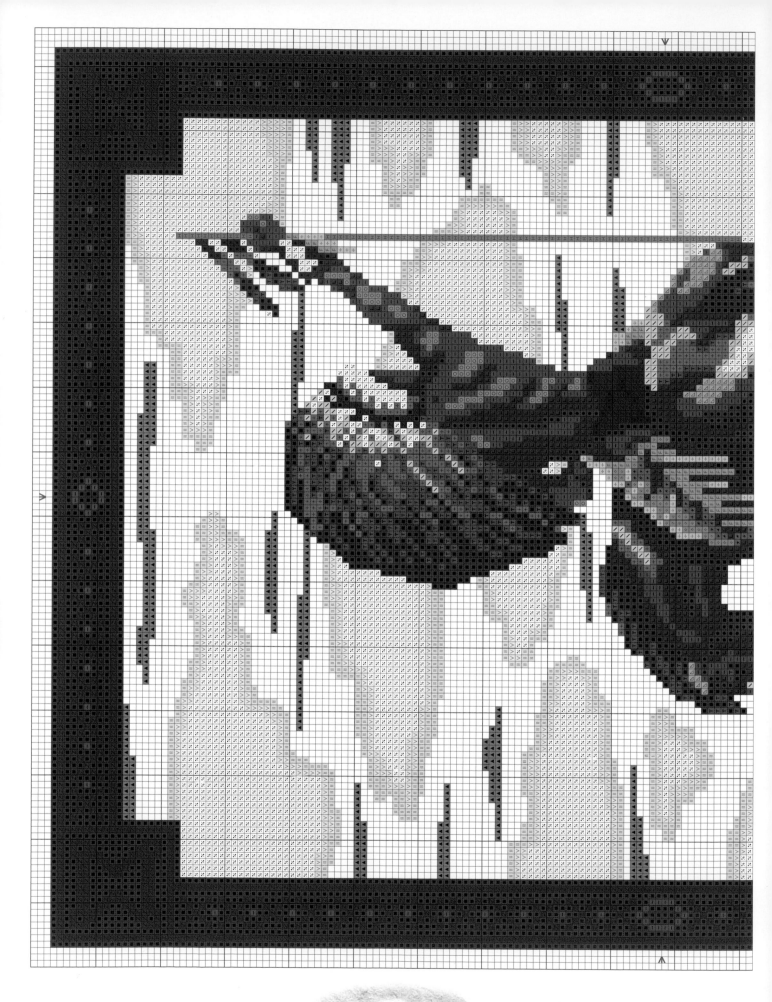

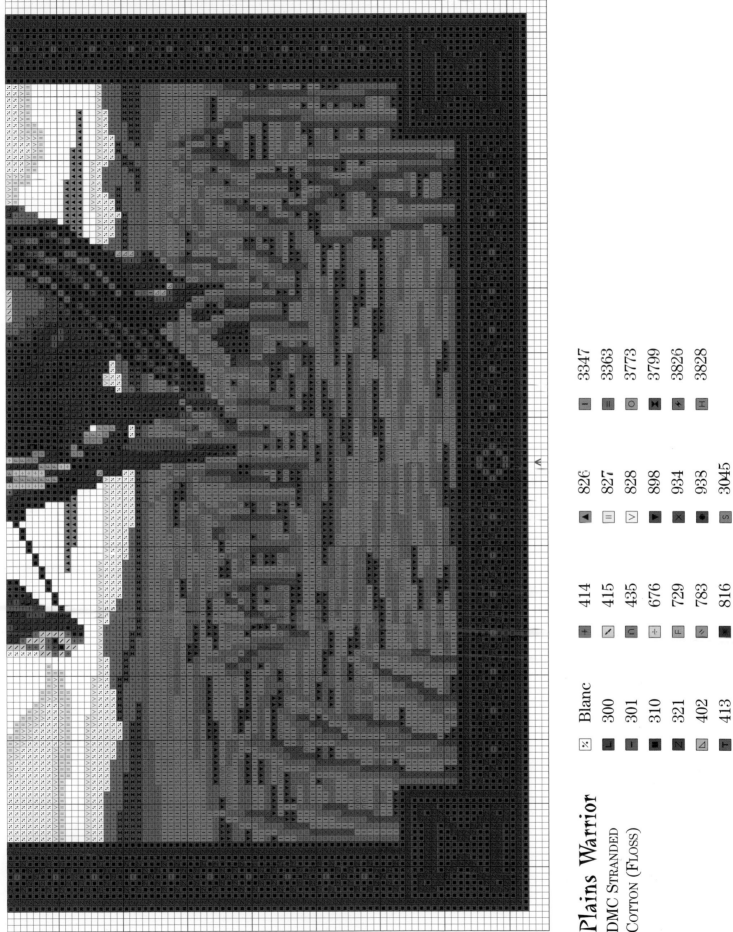

Plains Warrior

DMC STRANDED
COTTON (FLOSS)

☒	Blanc	◀	826	⊟	3347
⌐	300	⊟	827	⊟	3363
▮	301	▽	828	⊙	3773
▪	310	▶	898	✕	3799
N	321	✕	934	✦	3826
◿	402	◼	933	H	3828
T	413	s	3045		

+	414	
✓	415	
∩	435	
⊹	676	
F	729	
⁄	783	
✳	816	

Ceremonial Buffalo Skull

The buffalo were sacred to many Native American Indian tribes of the Great Plains. To the Sioux, the Buffalo embodied the power of the sun and its life-sustaining force. When they followed the buffalo on its migration, they believed they were following the sun on earth, which helped them to live in harmony with the sacred powers of the universe. Most Plains tribes used painted and decorated buffalo skulls in ceremonies to invoke the buffalo's sacred power, and songs, dances and ceremonies were offered for the successful renewal of the herds each year. Blackfeet and Dakota peoples painted buffalo skulls and stuffed the eye and nose cavities with sage and grass, as a symbolic offering to the buffalo to wish them successful grazing.

Now you can add an impressive buffalo skull design to a jacket or sweatshirt using waste canvas, or make your own Native American-style shoulder bag.

This ceremonial buffalo skull design can be stitched on many other items, including a tee-shirt, a sweat shirt, or a throw. It will look best set against a deep-coloured background. You could also add it to a shoulder bag you have bought using waste canvas, if you prefer not to make your own.

The jacket

Decorating clothing with a beautiful embroidery makes an unusual gift for someone special. Use waste canvas (see page 8) to apply the design to any fabric.

✧ Denim jacket or other clothing item of your choice
✧ Waste canvas, 14-count, 33.5 x 32cm (13¼ x 12⅝in)
✧ Tacking (basting) thread
✧ DMC stranded cotton (floss) in colours listed on chart
✧ Sharp or crewel needle
✧ Pair of fine tweezers
✧ Spray-bottle of water

1 Cut a piece of waste canvas about 4cm (1½in) wider and deeper than the finished size of your design.

2 Align the coloured threads in the waste canvas with the weave of the fabric on which you are stitching the design. Alternatively, align the waste canvas with a seam of the garment. Pin then tack (baste) the waste canvas into position as in fig. a.

fig. a Tacking waste canvas to the garment

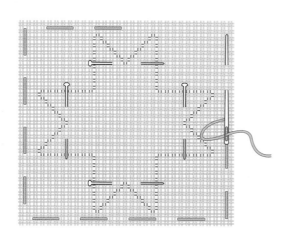

3 Treat each pair of canvas threads as a single thread, and stitch the design as you would on any evenweave fabric. Begin from the top and work downwards, follow-

fig. b Embroidering the design

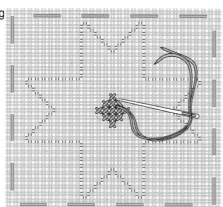

ing the chart on pages 44–45. Use two strands for the cross stitch and one strand for the backstitch, and work through the canvas and into the clothing fabric beneath as in fig. b.

4 Start and finish off the threads in the normal way by anchoring the starting thread under the first few stitches and by threading the finished ends under four or five stitches. If you are adding the motif to a garment that will be washed frequently, you may want to begin and end threads in a small knot for extra security.

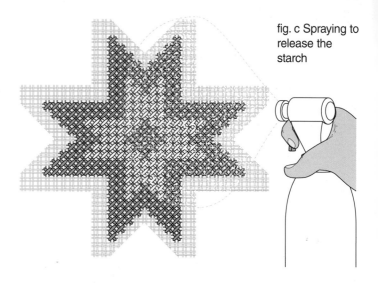

fig. c Spraying to release the starch

5 When you have completed the embroidery, cut away any excess canvas leaving 1.2cm (½in) all round the design. Lightly spray the embroidery with warm water.

fig. d Removing canvas threads

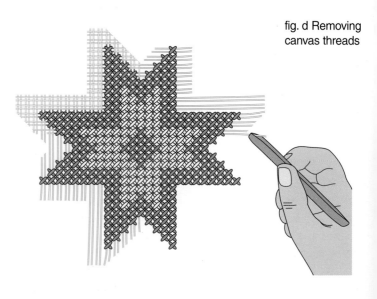

6 Use fine tweezers to pull out the canvas threads one by one as in fig. d. Resist the temptation to pull out more than one at a time – if you do, you may damage your embroidery. You may have to re-dampen your work from time to time to complete the task.

7 Place the finished piece right-side down on a soft, dry towel and press it lightly.

The shoulder bag

Make your own Native American-style shoulder bag stitched with repeats of the border design from the chart on pages 44 to 45.

✡ Colonial blue Aida fabric, 14-count, one 35 x 26cm (13¾ x 10¼in) piece and one, 111.5 x 16.7cm (44 x 6⅝in) strip
✡ Contrasting backing fabric, 35 x 26cm (13¾ x 10¼in)
✡ Two pieces of lining fabric, 35 x 26cm (13¾ x 10¼in)
✡ DMC stranded cotton (floss) in the colours listed on the chart
✡ Tapestry needle No 24
✡ Matching sewing thread
✡ Forty-nine deerskin laces, 10cm (4in) long
✡ Forty-nine 3cm (1⅛in) metal cones
✡ Craft adhesive

1 Prepare your fabric, find the starting point (see page 10) then, referring to the chart on page 45, stitch four rows of the repeating pattern down the bag front. Leave six blocks of unstitched fabric between each row and alternate the position of the motifs in each row as shown in the photograph. Line up the centre of the motifs across the top. On the shoulder strap piece, work from the centre out to each end of the strip starting and ending with a complete motif to continue the pattern on the bag front. Use two strands of stranded cotton (floss) throughout.

2 Place the completed front piece face down on a soft cloth or towel and press it carefully (see page 12).

3 Take the forty-nine deerskin laces, and thread the metal cones onto them (see page 14).

4 Place the embroidery right side up on a firm, flat surface, and apply craft adhesive to the end of each lace on the right side. Fix the laces side by side to the unstitched fabric of the seam allowance along one short edge, laying the laces with the right sides facing the right side of the embroidery.

5 Place the backing fabric on top, right sides facing, with the laces and cones sandwiched in between. Pin and tack (baste) along three edges, leaving the top edge open. Machine stitch along these three edges, using a 13mm (½in) seam allowance. Remove pins and tacking (basting) stitches.

6 Take the long Aida strip, and fold it in half lengthways with right sides facing, pin and tack (baste) together. Machine stitch together with a 13mm (½in) seam allowance. Remove pins and tacking (basting) stitches. Press seam open, and turn to the right side. Press, making sure that the embroidery is central.

7 With right sides together, place both ends of the shoulder strap on the top of the bag (with ends uppermost) against the seam, checking the embroidery on the handle is correctly positioned in relation to the embroidery on the bag. Pin and tack (baste) into place.

8 Put the two pieces of lining fabric together with right sides facing, pin and tack along both long edges and across the bottom, leaving a (5in) opening in the bottom for turning. Use a 13mm (½in) seam allowance. Machine stitch the tacked (basted) seams but DO NOT TURN the right way out at this point.

9 Clip any excess fabric from the corners on both the bag and the lining. Remove pins and tacking (basting) stitches. With right sides together, slip the embroidered bag inside the lining (keeping the side seams in line). Pin and tack (baste) the bag and lining together, all round the top, in a 1.5cm (½in) seam. Machine stitch the tacked (basted) seams, stitching through the ends of the shoulder strap as well. Trim the ends of the strap to 1.5cm (½in). Remove the pins and tacking (basting) stitches and turn to the right side, through the opening in the bottom of the lining.

10 Press in the seam allowance on the opening, and slip stitch to close. Push the lining into the bag.

If you stitch a design on a fabric that has to be dry cleaned, the canvas threads can be softened by rubbing them gently together. Take care to avoid damaging your stitches, but it should be possible to remove each canvas thread, one at a time, without having to use water.

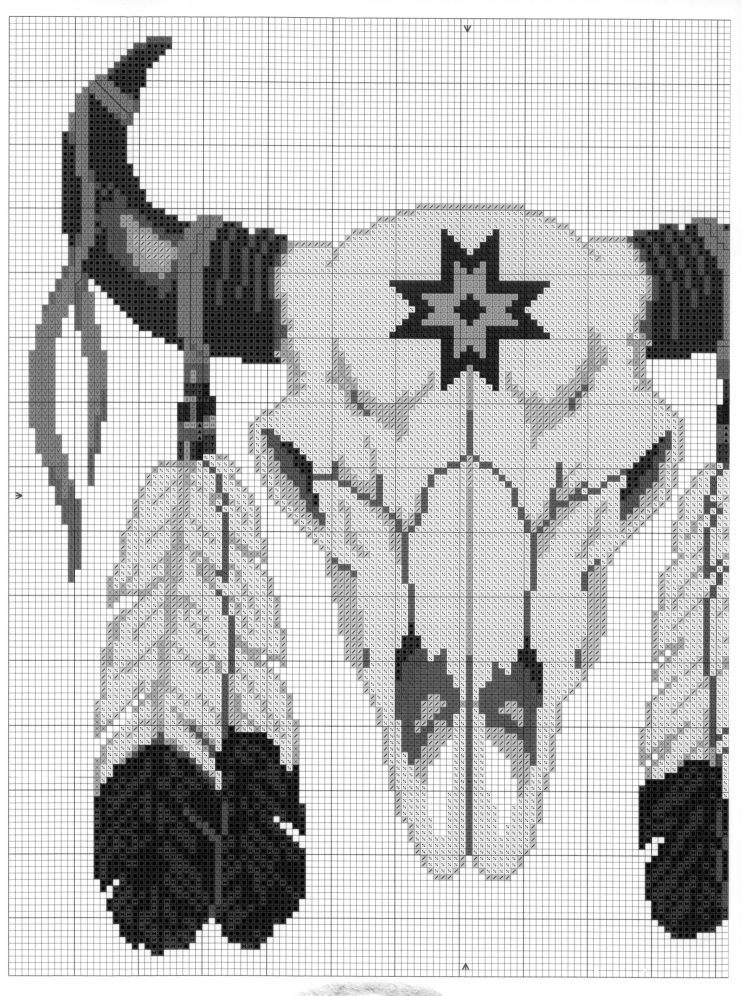

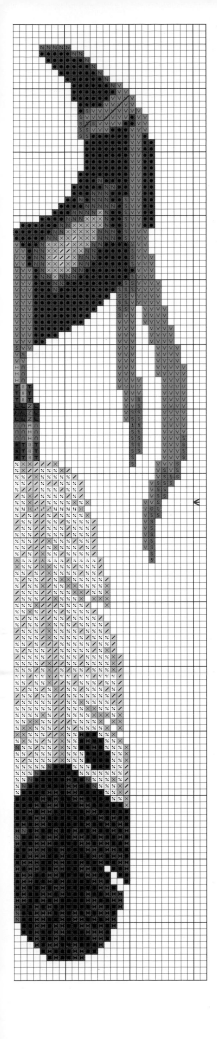

Shoulder bag motifs

Ceremonial Buffalo Skull

DMC STRANDED
COTTON (FLOSS)

Symbol	Colour
⊠	Blanc
−	307
■	310
N	317
✕	318
⋈	413
⹀	414
╱	415
▨	498
▟	666
S	781
V	783
T	797
‖	799
▧	820
∩	910
H	912
○	996
Z	3705
●	3799
▲	3818

Backstitch
╱ 780

Native American Indian Artefacts

Like every other civilisation, Native American Indians had objects that they treasured. I have brought together some of their beautifully-crafted artefacts in a cross stitch design. Some, like the ceremonial peace pipe smoked in the Chief's tipi, were at the heart of a social event. Others, like the bear claw amulet and the Shaman's medicine bag, were for protection. The Indians believed that wearing the bear's claws gave them the animal's strength. I have decorated my medicine bag with a painted Thunderbird, known as the sacred bearer of happiness. Bear tracks like the one in the top right corner, were painted on tipis and war shields. The last artefact in the picture, the war club, has a mountain lion print beside it.

The framed picture

Stitch the whole Artefacts chart to make a stunning framed picture, or take individual elements of the design to make smaller items.

✡ White Hardanger fabric, 22-count, 47.5 x 43cm (18¾ x 17in)
✡ DMC stranded cotton (floss) in the colours listed on the chart
✡ Tapestry needle, No 26
✡ Firm mounting board, 40 x 35.5cm (15¾ x 14in)
✡ Masking tape
✡ Picture frame of your choice

1 Prepare your fabric and find the starting point (see page 10). Then, following the Native American Indian Artefacts chart on pages 48–51, work the design downwards. Stitch with one strand of stranded cotton (floss) throughout.

2 When you have completed the embroidery, place it face down on a soft cloth or towel and press it carefully (see page 12).

3 See 'Mounting embroideries for framing' on page 12 to mount and frame the finished embroidery.

Greetings card

Stitch the ceremonial pipe from the main chart to go in a card mount you have decorated yourself.

✡ Silver-fleck Bellana fabric, 20-count, 17.3 x 15.7cm (6⅞ x 6¼in)
✡ DMC stranded cotton (floss) in the colours listed on the chart
✡ Tapestry needle, No 26
✡ Thin card in a colour of your choice 42 x 23cm (16½ x 9in) (available from art shops or some stationers)
✡ Contrasting thin card 21 x 19cm (8¼ x 7½in)
✡ Medium-weight iron-on interfacing (optional)
✡ Double-sided adhesive tape
✡ Scalpel or craft knife
✡ Black indelible ink art pen (available from art shops or craft suppliers)

1 Prepare your fabric, find the starting point (see page 10) then, following the chosen figure from the chart on pages 48 to 51, work the design downwards. Use one strand of stranded cotton (floss) throughout.

2 When you have completed the embroidery, place it face down on a soft cloth or towel and press it carefully (see page 12). Then, iron the interfacing to the wrong side.

3 Make a fold-line dividing the larger piece of thin card into two equal sections by measuring 21cm (8¼in) along the width and lightly marking a line on the wrong side. Using the scalpel or craft knife, cut an aperture 15 x 13cm (6 x 5¼in) from the left-hand section. With the back of the blade, gently score the fold-line previously marked.

4 Transfer your chosen designs from the black and white line drawings on page 122 (see 'Transferring motifs on to card mounts' on page 14) onto the card mount, and draw over them using the black pen. See page 13 for mounting embroidery in a card.

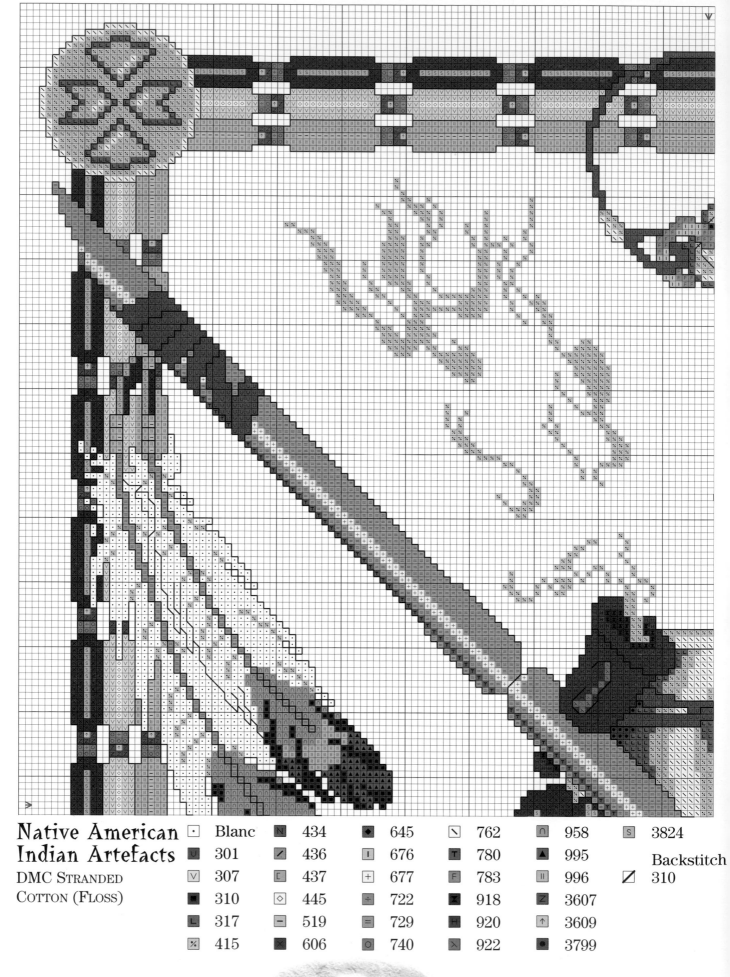

Native American Indian Artefacts

DMC STRANDED COTTON (FLOSS)

⊡	Blanc	N	434	◆	645	◥	762	∩	958	S	3824		
⊍	301	⁄	436	I	676	T	780	▲	995			**Backstitch**	
V	307	⊏	437	+	677	F	783	‖	996	⁄	310		
■	310	◇	445	÷	722	⊠	918	Z	3607				
L	317	−	519	=	729	H	920	↑	3609				
⁒	415	⊠	606	○	740	◺	922	▣	3799				

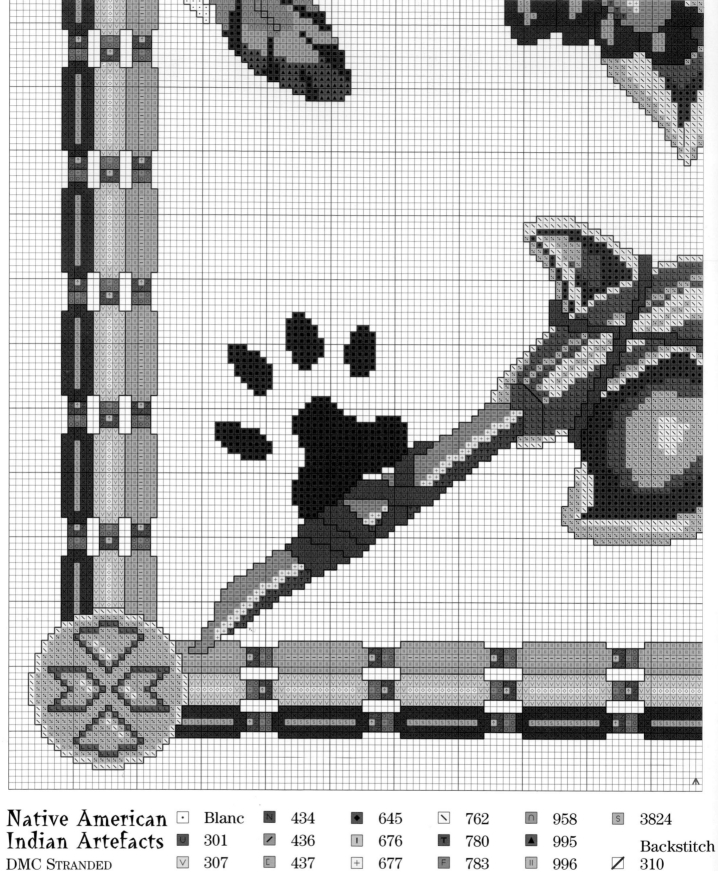

Native American Indian Artefacts

DMC Stranded Cotton (Floss)

·	Blanc	N	434	◆	645	⧅	762	∩	958	S	3824
U	301	⁄	436	I	676	T	780	‖	995		
V	307	L	437	+	677	F	783	‖	996		**Backstitch**
■	310	◇	445	÷	722	✖	918	Z	3607	⧄	310
L	317	–	519	=	729	⋈	920	↑	3609		
⅛	415	✕	606	O	740	λ	922	⬢	3799		

The Natural World

Native American Indians believed that the Earth belonged to everyone, that it was their mother who gave them life. To them, it was important to live in harmony with their world, since the Earth provided everything they needed to survive. They never sought to control nature; instead they respected it and were grateful for the blessings it gave them. They could not understand why the Pilgrims built fences because they did not believe that the Earth could be owned. Their myths, rituals and art reflect these beliefs.

Many Native American Indians believe that animals, birds and plants are children of the Earth which must not be used, but should be treated with respect. In some tribes, hunters say a prayer before killing an animal: 'Forgive me, brother, but my people must eat'.

From the coyote picture and the eagle crest to the floral beadwork patterns, the designs in this section reflect this respect for the natural world. Both the Sioux warrior in the opening portrait, and the brave in the 'End of the Trail' picture illustrate the strength of the relationship between Indian man and his horse.

This large and dramatic portrait of a Sioux warrior will grab the attention of everyone who sees it. With every square of the massive chart filled in, it's not a project for the faint-hearted, but the finished design makes it well worth all that hard work.

Sioux Warrior

The Sioux were a proud and strong Native American Indian nation. The Dakotas, one branch of this large and complex tribe, lived off the land between the forks of the Missouri and the Mississippi. They could never accept the demands of the white people who were moving onto their land in ever-increasing numbers. Little by little, the Native American Indians were forced to give up one area after another of their country to the Government. In the face of such hardship and provocation, the Dakotas showed themselves to be capable of great loyalty and heroism. When forced to fight to defend their hunting grounds, the warriors proved themselves brave and skilful in battle; and the battle expertise of their chiefs won the admiration of those who fought against them.

This portrait celebrates the skill and courage of the Dakota Sioux warriors.

The word Sioux is a corruption, made by the early French settlers, of the Algonquin word 'Nadouessioux', meaning 'snakes'. It was also the Chippewa name for their 'adders' or 'enemies'. The Sioux people's own name for themselves is Ocheti Shakowin, the 'Seven Council Fires', or seven tribes that originally formed their nation.

The portrait

You will probably find it helpful to mark off the stitches on this dense chart as you work them, on an enlarged photocopy.

✡ White Aida fabric, 14-count, 71 x 55cm (28 x 21¾in)
✡ DMC stranded cotton (floss) in the colours listed on the chart
✡ Tapestry needle, No 24
✡ Firm mounting board, 63.5 x 47.5cm (25 x 18¾in)
✡ Masking tape
✡ Picture frame of your choice

1 Prepare your fabric, find the starting point (see page 10) then, following the Sioux Warrior chart on pages 56 to 59, work the design downwards. Use two strands of stranded cotton (floss) throughout.

2 When you have completed the embroidery, place it face down on a soft cloth or towel and press it carefully (see page 12).

3 See 'Mounting embroideries for framing' on page 12 to mount and frame the finished embroidery.

Pencil case

If you prefer to stitch a smaller project instead of the whole portrait, take the border motifs to decorate a pencil case.

✡ White Aida fabric, 14-count, 12.5 x 28cm (5 x 11in)
✡ Contrasting backing fabric, 12.5 x 28cm (5 x 11in)
✡ DMC stranded cotton (floss) in the colours listed on the chart
✡ Tapestry needle, No 24
✡ Plastic lining, 16.5 x 23cm (6½ x 9in)
✡ Zip fastener, 20.5cm (8in) long
✡ Matching sewing thread
Measurements include a 13mm (½in) seam allowance

1 Prepare your fabric, find the starting point (see page 10) then, following the border design from the bottom edge of the Sioux Warrior chart on pages 56 to 59, work the design downwards. Your embroidery should be 20cm (7⅛in) wide. Stitch two pattern repeats from the side border design for the tab. Use two strands of stranded cotton (floss) throughout, and remember to position the designs on the fabric to allow enough space all round for the seam allowances.

2 When you have completed the embroidery, place it face down on a soft cloth or towel and press it carefully (see page 12).

3 Cut out the finished embroideries allowing a 13mm (½in) seam allowance all round. Cut the backing material to the same size.

4 Take the pencil case embroidered front, and with right sides together, pin and tack (baste) one side of the zip fastener to the top edge of the Aida. Machine stitch together, keeping the seam 5mm (¼in) away from the zip. Stitch the other side of the zip to the backing material in the same way. Remove pins and tacking (basting) stitches.

5 To make the tab, place the embroidered work and the backing right sides together, and stitch along the edge down both long sides. Trim the stitched seams to 1cm (¼in) leaving 13mm (⅜in) allowance on both short edges. Turn to the right side and press.

6 With right sides together, stitch one end of the tab to the Aida close to the embroidery on the front, and the other side to the backing fabric, just below the zip.

7 Take the plastic lining, and place one long edge over the zip tape, so that the zip is between the plastic and the embroidery, ensuring the top edges are level. Stitch along the previous stitching line on the zip tape, with the plastic underneath. Place a piece of tissue paper under the plastic if you experience difficulty with machining. Stitch the other side of the plastic to the backing in the same way. Trim the seams to the edge of the zip tape.

8 Pin and tack (baste) the embroidered work to the backing along the two short edges catching in the tab, and across the bottom edge, leaving a 7.5cm (3in) opening in the bottom seam for turning.

9 With the seam of the zip towards the embroidery, stitch along the short sides of the plastic lining, then stitch the embroidery and backing fabric together along the tacked (basted) seam. Remove pins and tacking (basting) stitches, trim the seams and clip any excess fabric from the corners. Turn to the right side through the opening in the bottom edge, turn in the seam allowance on the opening, and slip stitch to close.

This unusual pencil case uses the border design from the chart on pages 57-59 to create a colourful and useful piece

Sioux Warrior

DMC STRANDED
COTTON (FLOSS)

▲	Blanc		801
▣	300	✎	809
⊙	301	▧	814
▦	304	▨	815
■	310	⊤	816
⊟	311	⊕	817
✚	312	▨	820
⊿	315	♠	823
L	316	✳	838
⊗	317	⊘	839
⦂	318	▷	840
⬆	321	♡	869
Z	322	✷	895
→	334	⊞	898
●	336	⌷	900
✦	349	⊞	902
U	407	◪	905
✦	413	⌂	919
✕	414	◀	924
⋏	415	⊠	938
✵	433	⌐	947
▶	444	I	950
▣	498	⊡	972
⊞	501	%	973
⌂	606	◪	975
◣	610	V	976
✖	632	–	995
⊞	646	O	996
⌐	647	◈	3021
✳	666	N	3064
<	676	⋀	3354
▣	677	✳	3371
⊂	720	◱	3705
‖	729	✚	3722
←	741	⋅	3755
T	742	⬉	3761
✚	780	▢	3772
◥	782	⌐	3787
▽	783	⊃	3799
▣	796	⊿	3826
S	798		

Sioux Warrior

DMC STRANDED COTTON (FLOSS)

▲	Blanc		801
	300		809
	301		814
	304		815
	310		816
	311		817
	312		820
	315		823
L	316		838
⊗	317		839
⦂	318		840
	321		869
Z	322		895
→	334		898
	336		900
	349		902
U	407		905
	413		919
✕	414		924
⋋	415		938
	433		947
▶	444		950
	498		972
	501		973
	606		975
	610	▽	976
	632	−	995
H	646	○	996
⌐	647		3021
★	666	N	3064
<	676	∧	3354
	677		3371
C	720		3705
‖	729		3722
←	741	·	3755
T	742	⌐	3761
	780		3772
	782		3787
▽	783		3799
S	796	△	3826
S	798		

End of The Trail

As the setting sun turns the incredible Arizona landscape blood-red, an Apache Indian and his horse rest for a moment on a rocky outcrop. They have covered many miles since sunup and they are exhausted – they might have been travelling for days. The horse takes the opportunity to graze while his master sinks forward in repose. They have a special bond which keeps them going, and at this moment, horse and rider are as one.

The End of the Trail is a popular Native American image, which inspired me to design a picture illustrating the closeness of the Indian brave and his horse. It is framed by a floral border on a dark background.

Framed picture

A rich coloured wooden frame sets off this picture very well. The design is stitched on 16-count aida.

- ✡ Cream Aida fabric, 16-count, 47 x 39.5cm (18½ x 15½in)
- ✡ DMC stranded cotton (floss) in the colours listed on the chart
- ✡ Tapestry needle, No 26
- ✡ Firm mounting board, 39.5 x 32cm (15½ x 12½in)
- ✡ Masking tape
- ✡ Picture frame of your choice

1 Prepare your fabric, find the starting point (see page 10) then, following the End of Trail chart on pages 62 and 63, work the design downwards. Use two strands of stranded cotton (floss) throughout.

2 When you have completed the embroidery, place it face down on a soft cloth or towel and press it carefully (see page 12).

3 See 'Mounting embroideries for framing' on page 12 to mount and frame the finished embroidery.

Greetings card

Stitch the Apache brave on his own to go in an original card decorated with Native American line drawings taken from the Pictographs on page 122.

- ✡ Sky blue Aida fabric, 18-count, 18.2 x 17cm (7¼ x 6¾in)
- ✡ DMC stranded cotton (floss) in the colours listed on the chart
- ✡ Tapestry needle, No. 26
- ✡ Thin card in a colour of your choice, 47.5 x 25.3cm (18¾ x 10in)
- ✡ Contrasting thin card, 23 x 21cm (9¼ x 8¼in)
- ✡ Medium-weight iron-on interfacing (optional)
- ✡ Double-sided adhesive tape
- ✡ Scalpel or craft knife
- ✡ Black indelible-ink art pen

1 Prepare your fabric, find the starting point (see page 10) then, following the horse and brave on the chart on pages 62 and 63, work the design downwards. Use two strands of stranded cotton (floss) throughout.

2 Place your completed embroidery face down on a soft cloth or towel and press carefully (see page 12). Iron the interfacing to the wrong side if using.

3 See page 46, point 3 for how to cut out your card: it should have an aperture of 15 x 13.5cm (6 x 5⅜in). See 'Transferring motifs on to card mounts' on page 14, and 'Mounting embroidery in a card' on page 13.

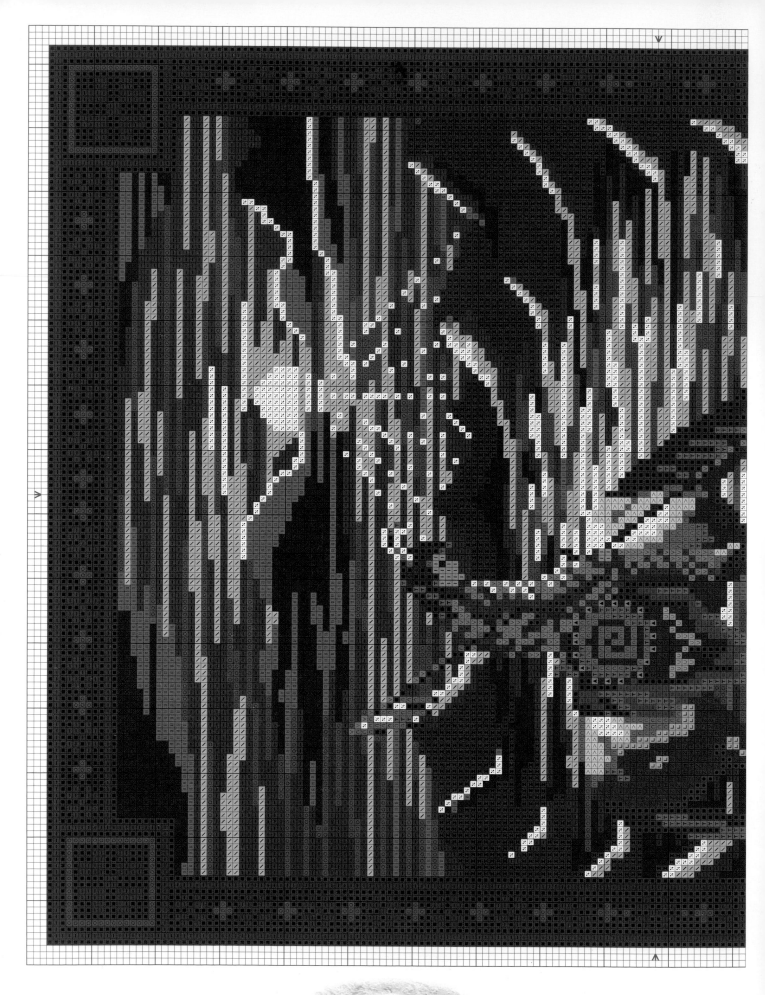

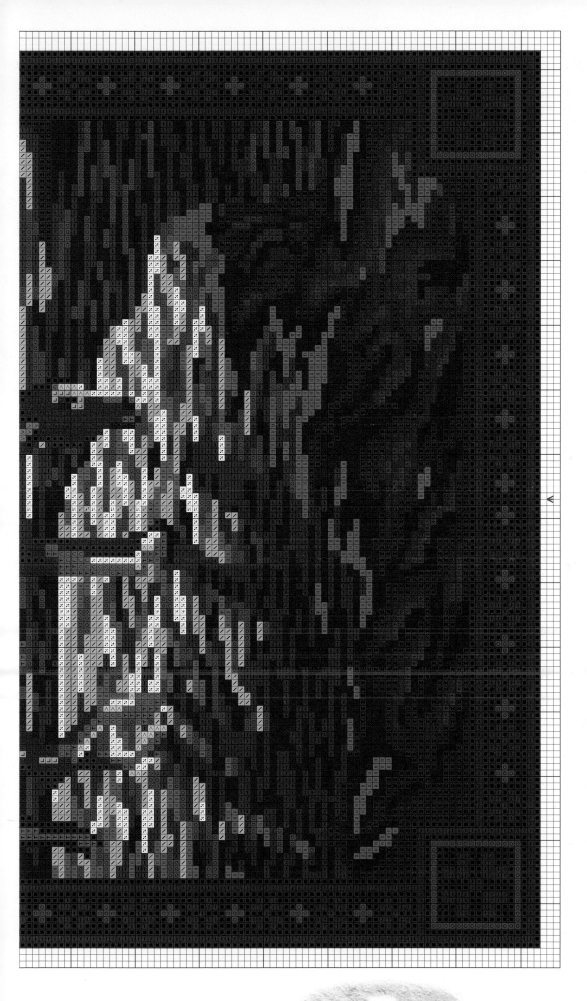

End of
The Trail

DMC Stranded
Cotton (Floss)

⊠	Blanc		⊙	720	∨	3045
N	300		⊞	838	–	3064
s	304		⊞	919	⊠	3371
■	310		←	920	N	3772
⊤	317		●	938	⊪	3799
I	326		◀	3012	⁄	3824
L	402					
C	414					
⋗	415					
⊔	436					
⊠	550					
⊫	553					

Eagle Crest

To the Native Americans the eagle was a highly symbolic bird and it often features in their stories and drawings. I based this design on an Eagle crest from the Haida Tribe of the North-west coast of America. It originally appeared on a wooden drum, painted in black and red. A series of thick and thin painted outlines create the form of the eagle even including some of the bird's internal organs.

The sweatshirt

The eagle crest stands out well on a white sweatshirt. Use waste canvas to add cross stitch motifs to clothing.

- ✤ Sweatshirt or other clothing item of your choice
- ✤ Waste canvas, 14-count, 34.5 x 31cm (13⅝ x 12¼in)
- ✤ Tacking (basting) thread
- ✤ DMC stranded cotton (floss) in colours listed on chart
- ✤ Tapestry needle, No 24
- ✤ Pair of fine tweezers
- ✤ Spray-bottle of water

1 Cut a piece of waste canvas about 4cm (1½in) wider and deeper than the finished design size will be.

2 Align the coloured threads in the waste canvas with the weave of the garment fabric or align the canvas with a seam. Pin then tack (baste) into position.

3 Stitch the chart on pages 66–67, using two strands for the cross stitch and one strand for the backstitch, and following the waste canvas instructions on page 42.

The striking Eagle Crest can be stitched on clothing using waste canvas or made into a framed picture. Here it has been stitched in one strand on 22-count mulberry aida. With only two colours used throughout the design, it is very easy to substitute your own choice of fabric and thread colours.

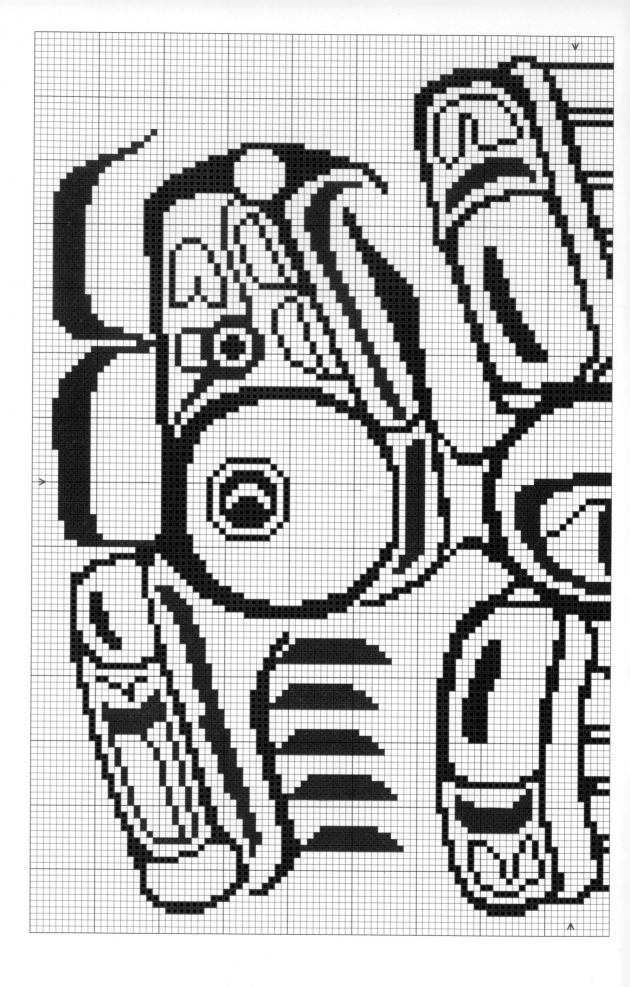

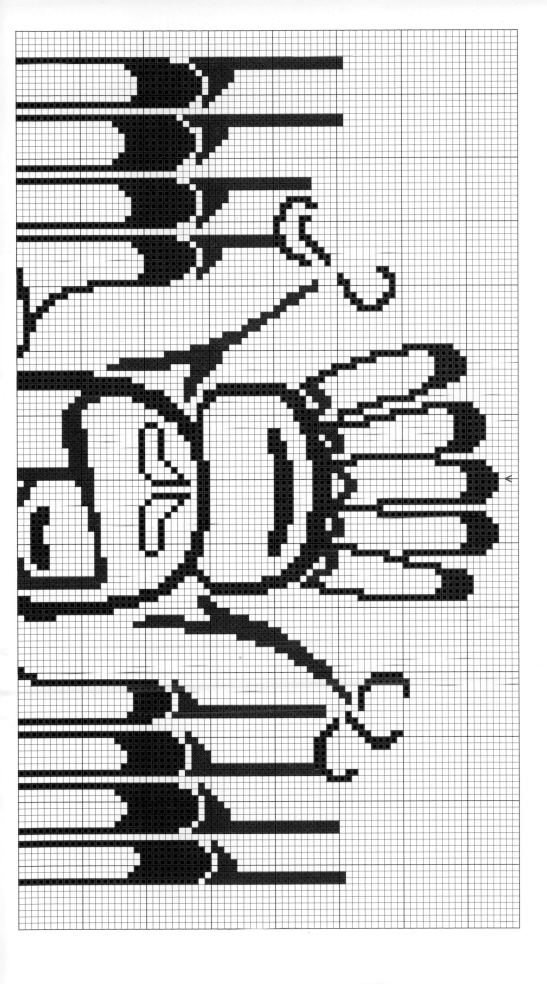

Eagle Crest
DMC STRANDED COTTON (FLOSS)

- ■ 310
- ⊠ 666

Coyote

According to legend, Coyote created the
world and the creatures in it. He held a
council of animals to discuss how to
choose the Lord of the Animals. After
much argument, Coyote decided they
should all make a model of the Lord of the
Animals from river mud, and choose the
best one. When darkness fell, the animals
slept, leaving their models unfinished.
The crafty Coyote remained awake all
night, and made his model by moonlight.
The lapping river washed away the other
animals' unfinished models.

Early in the morning Coyote finished his
model and gave him life. The result: a
superior being who could hear the slight-
est sound, and see far into the distance.
Like a bear, he stood on two legs, and his
voice was tuneful. Like a fish, his skin
was smooth and he swam in the sea.

This superior being was the Native
American Indian, Lord of the Animals,
cunning and clever – like a coyote.

Framed picture
Stitch a beautiful picture of the cunning coyote, and
decorate the frame with American Indian Conchos
and a Lobo Bolo slide.

✿ Navy Aida fabric, 14-count, 43.5 x 35.5cm (17¼ x 14in)
✿ DMC stranded cotton (floss) in the colours listed on the chart
✿ Tapestry needle, No 24
✿ Firm mounting board, 36 x 28cm (14¼ x 11in)
✿ Masking tape
✿ Picture frame of your choice
✿ One Lobo Bolo slide
✿ Four enamelled spot conchos
✿ Two-pack epoxy resin
✿ Small pair of side cutters
✿ Precision needle file

1 Prepare your fabric, find the starting point (see page
10) then, following the Coyote chart on pages 70 and
71, work the design downwards. Use two strands of
stranded cotton (floss) throughout.

2 Place your completed embroidery face down on a
soft cloth or towel and press carefully (see page 12).

3 See 'Mounting embroideries for framing' on page 12
to mount and frame the finished embroidery.

4 To decorate the frame, cut the Lobo Bolo slide clip,
and back prongs off with side cutters, filing down
any protruding metal with the needle file. Then fix the
slide and the conchos to the frame with epoxy resin.

Greetings card
Stitch the coyote to go in a card decorated with line
drawings taken from the Pictographs on page 122.

✿ Sky blue Aida fabric, 18-count, 20cm x 14.5cm (8 x 5¾in)
✿ DMC stranded cotton (floss) in the colours listed on the chart
✿ Tapestry needle, No. 26
✿ Thin card in a colour of your choice, 43 x 26cm (17 x 10¼in)
✿ Contrasting thin card, 24 x 20cm (9½ x 7⅞in)
✿ Double-sided adhesive tape
✿ Scalpel or craft knife
✿ Black indelible ink art pen

1 Find the starting point on your fabric (see page 10)
and work the coyote downwards from the chart on
pages 70–71. Use two strands of stranded cotton (floss).
Refer to points 2-4 on page 46 for how to make the card,
which needs an aperture of 15.6 x 11.3cm (6¼ x 4½in).

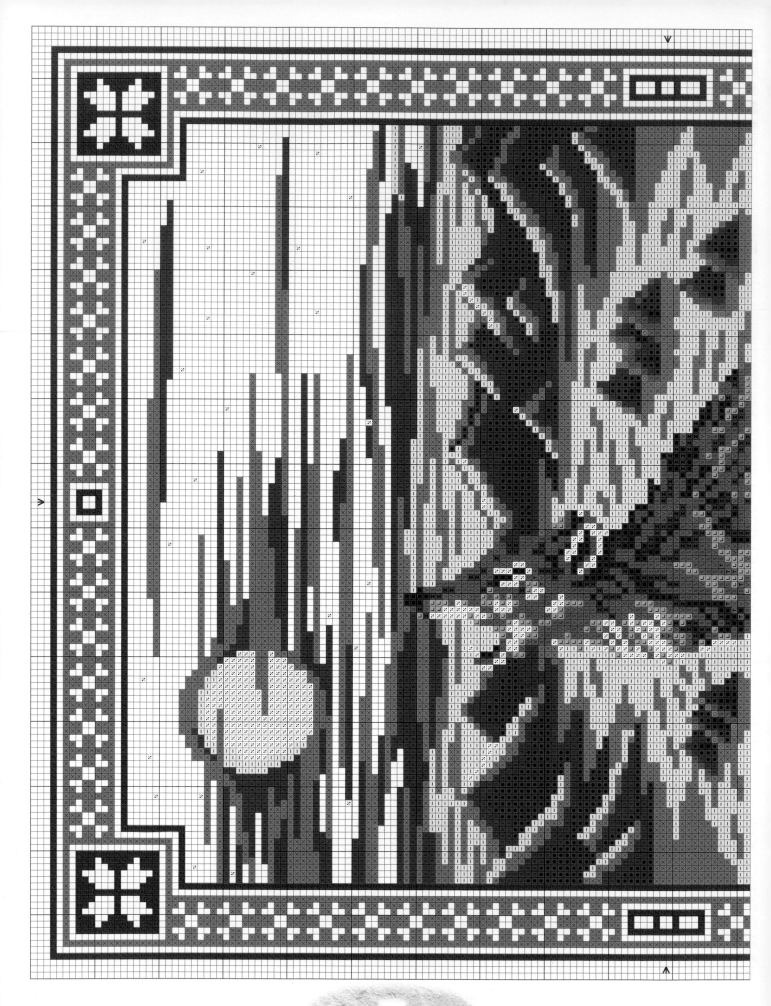

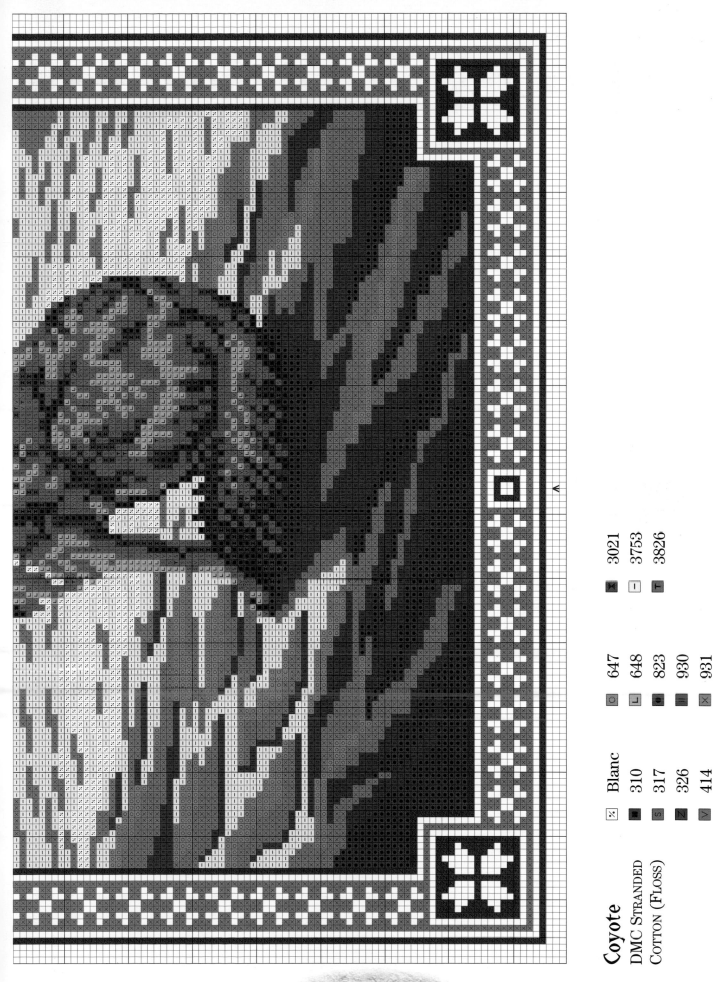

Coyote

DMC STRANDED
COTTON (FLOSS)

✕ Blanc	⊙ 647	✖ 3021
■ 310	∟ 648	⊡ 3753
▨ 317	⬢ 823	⊤ 3826
▣ 326	▤ 930	
⋁ 414	✕ 931	

Ute Floral Designs

Native American Indians took the inspiration for some of their intricate beadwork patterns from the plants and flowers they saw around them. These floral designs are in the style of beadwork made by tribes from the Plateau and Basin, North-east, and Sub-Arctic areas. The strong repeating motifs are ideal for decorating clothing.

The design stitched on the shirt cuffs is based on a Chippewa woven beadwork design from a buckskin belt. The smaller design stitched on the shirt pocket, is from the cover of a cradleboard used by a Cree woman to carry her baby around at the end of the nineteenth century. The third design which appears on the lavender sachet, is from a doeskin tobacco pouch made by the Thompson Indians.

Embroidered shirt

Liven up a plain shirt, by buying some waste canvas, and decorating it with cross stitched motifs.

- ✿ Plain cotton shirt
- ✿ Waste canvas, 14-count, two 6.5 x 20cm (2½ x 8in) pieces for the cuffs and one 9 x 12.5cm (3½ x 5in) piece for the pocket
- ✿ Tacking (basting) thread
- ✿ DMC stranded cotton (floss) in the colours listed on the chart
- ✿ Sharp or crewel needle
- ✿ Pair of fine tweezers
- ✿ Spray-bottle of water

1 For each motif, cut your waste canvas 4cm (1½in) wider and deeper than the finished design will be.

2 Align the coloured threads in the waste canvas with the weave of the shirt, or, align the waste canvas with a seam of the garment. Pin, then tack (baste) the waste canvas into position.

3 Stitch the Chippewa design on the shirt cuffs and the Cree design on the pocket from the chart on page 74, following the waste canvas instructions for the Ceremonial Buffalo Skull project on page 42. Use two strands for the cross stitch. You will probably find it easier to unpick the stitches and remove the pocket from the shirt before you start.

Lavender sachet

Keep your clothes smelling sweet, by making this pretty sachet to place in your drawer.

- ✿ Peach Hardanger fabric, 22-count, 13 x 15cm (5¼ x 6in)
- ✿ Contrasting backing fabric, 13 x 15cm (5¼ x 6in)
- ✿ DMC stranded cotton (floss) in the colours listed on the chart
- ✿ Four tassels in a matching colour (see page 14)
- ✿ Four black pony beads
- ✿ Matching sewing thread
- ✿ Tapestry needle, No 26
- ✿ Small amount of kapok or polyester filling
- ✿ Small amount of lavender

Measurements include a 1.3cm (½in) seam allowance

1 Prepare your fabric, find the starting point (see page 10) then, following the Thompson Indians chart on page 74, work the design downwards. Use one strand of stranded cotton (floss) throughout.

2 Lay your completed embroidery face down on a soft cloth or towel and press carefully (see page 12).

3 Place your embroidery right side up on a firm, flat surface with the backing fabric on top, right sides together. Pin and tack (baste) three sides of the sachet.

4 Machine stitch the tacked (basted) seams and clip the excess fabric from the corners. Remove the pins and tacking (basting) stitches and turn to the right side.

5 Stuff the sachet firmly, adding the lavender with the filling. Turn in the seam allowance on the open edge and slip stitch to close, adding small amounts of filling as you go. Thread a pony bead onto each tassel if desired, and hand-stitch a tassel to each corner.

Cree

Thompson Indians

Chippewa

Floral Designs

DMC Stranded Cotton (Floss)

⊙	225	S	632	T	931	Z	996	▽	3773
■	310	N	703	‖	972	◣	3346		
✕	334	+	726	▬	975	L	3726		
◹	561	↑	823	⁒	977	·	3755		
↗	606	═	890	U	988	✳	3761		

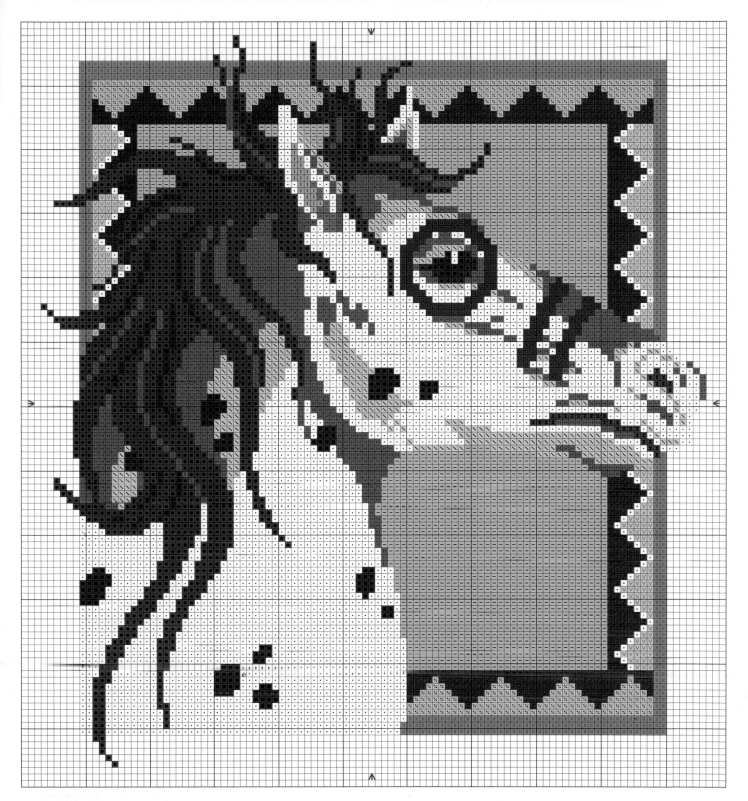

Sioux Horse Cushion

DMC STRANDED
COTTON (FLOSS)

⊡	Blanc	⊞	414	▨	820
▲	300	◺	415	‖	988
▪	310	▣	498	−	996
▩	317	◔	666	▨	3727
=	356	⋁	726	●	3799
✳	413	▯	758		

Sioux Horse

The Spaniards took horses to America and traded them with the Native Indian tribes. By the mid-1800s, most Plains Indian tribes had horses and the braves learnt to be skilled and fearless horse-men. Horses became a symbol of wealth and status, but the daring horse raids carried out by tribes on their neighbours also made them a cause of warfare.

I took the inspiration for this stylised cushion design from an old Sioux custom. The Sioux warrior would paint red or white coup lines across his horse's nose to show how many times it had been into battle, and red or white circles around its eyes. They believed this would improve the animal's vision in hunting and in war. The border and the background design is from a Sioux beaded knife sheath dated 1875–1900.

You may not be able to find cushion pads of the desired size in the shops, but you can follow the 3 easy steps on page 100 to make your own.

The cushion

Make a stunning cushion stitched in vibrant colours on a bright red background.

✿ Christmas-red Aida fabric, 14-count, 31.5 x 29.5cm (12½ x 11⅝in)
✿ Contrasting backing fabric, 31.5 x 29.5cm (12½ x 11⅝in)
✿ DMC stranded cotton (floss) in the colours listed on the chart
✿ Tapestry needle, No 24
✿ Matching sewing thread
✿ Cushion pad, 29 x 26.7cm (11½ x 10⅝in)
✿ Four tassels to match the embroidery
✿ Twelve pony beads in colours to complement the embroidery
Measurements include a 13mm (½in) seam allowance

1 Prepare your fabric, find the starting point (see page 10) then, following the Sioux Horse chart on page 75, work the design downwards. Use two strands of stranded cotton (floss) throughout.

2 When you have completed the embroidery, place it face down on a soft cloth or towel and press it carefully (see page 12).

3 Place your embroidery right side up on a firm, flat surface, with the backing fabric on top, right sides together. Pin and tack (baste) three sides of the cushion.

4 Machine-stitch the tacked (basted) seams and then clip excess fabric from the corners. Remove the pins and tacking (basting) stitches, and turn to the right side.

5 Thread three pony beads on to each tassel (see page 14 for how to make a tassel), and hand-stitch a tassel to each corner. Press in the seam allowance along each side of the opening. Place the cushion pad inside the cover, and oversew the edges together.

Native Arts and Crafts

Native American Indians were gifted artists, who made practical yet beautifully-crafted everyday objects. Their painting, carving and embroidery contained many stories and often referred to the spirits in the images they used. Their arts and crafts are the result of a long tradition by which such skills as pottery, silversmithing, wood carving, beading and weaving were passed down from one generation to another.

As the artists' tools were limited, they would use simple materials but include intricate designs. Much Native American art is symbolic, but a lot is decorative, too. Men painted, made pipes and did rock carving, while women, who were very skilled at needlework, decorated clothes, bags or belts with exquisite embroidery, beadwork or quillwork.

Today, artists and craftspeople recreate these Native American arts and crafts using vibrant colours and modern materials. The projects in this section show how strong such designs can be. There's a bold geometric Navajo rug, a symbolic sand painting throw and some stylish tasselled cushions. But first, there's the portrait of a Nez Perce tribeswoman.

This striking portrait of a Nez Perce tribeswoman would make a vibrant centrepiece for a room. Mounting it in a dark, ornate wooden frame sets off the bright colours in the design very well.

Nez Perce Tribeswoman

The portrait of the magnificently-dressed Nez Perce tribeswoman photographed on page 78 shows off many of the skills of Native American artists and craftsmen in the vibrantly-coloured clothes and beautiful jewellery she is wearing. She wears a belted deerskin dress decorated with a heavily-beaded yolk in the Plains style and edged with long fringes, and she is holding a cornhusk friendship bag with an abstract floral beadwork design. She wears long loops of bead and shell necklaces, a pony bead and abalone shell choker, shell earrings, and brass bracelets. Her hair is worn in two braids, wrapped in otter fur.

The portrait

Stitch the whole portrait or take elements from the chart and turn them into a pouch and a purse.

✿ White Aida, 14-count, 71 x 55cm (28 x 21¾in)
✿ DMC stranded cotton (floss) in the colours listed on the chart
✿ Tapestry needle, No 24
✿ Picture frame of your choice

1 Prepare your fabric, find the starting point (see page 10) then, following the Nez Perce Tribeswoman chart on pages 82–85, work the design downwards. Use two strands of stranded cotton (floss) throughout.

2 When you have completed the embroidery, place it face down on a soft cloth or towel and press it carefully. See 'Mounting embroideries for framing' on page 12 for advice on how to mount and frame the finished embroidery.

Small pouch

Taking the friendship bag from the chart on page 82, and stitching it as a design on its own, you can make a pretty pouch to hang round your neck.

✿ White Aida fabric, 18-count, 9.5 x 10cm (3¾ x 4in)
✿ Contrasting backing fabric, 9.5 x 10cm (3¾ x 4in)
✿ Medium-weight iron-on interfacing, 9.5 x 10cm (3¾ x 4in)
✿ DMC stranded cotton (floss) in the colours listed on the chart
✿ Tapestry needle No 26
✿ Matching sewing thread
✿ One deerskin lace, 91.5cm (36in) long
✿ Four pony beads in colours to complement the embroidery

1 Prepare your fabric, find the starting point (see page 10) then, following the bag design from the chart on pages 82–85, work the design downwards. Use two strands of stranded cotton (floss) throughout.

2 Press the finished embroidery face down on a soft cloth or towel (see page 12). Then, iron the interfacing on to the wrong side.

3 Place the embroidery right side up on a firm, flat surface with the backing fabric on top, right sides together. Pin and tack (baste) along three edges, leaving the top edge open and allowing for a 2cm (¾in) seam, and leaving a strip of unworked Aida the width of the deerskin lace at each side of the embroidery.

4 Machine-stitch the tacked (basted) seams, and then machine-stitch another row of stitching, 7mm (¼in) away from the first row. Trim the seam close to the stitching and clip any excess fabric from the corners.

5 Neaten the edge of the Aida and backing fabric on the top, and slip stitch into place. Remove the pins and tacking (basting) stitches, and turn to the right side.

6 Take the deerskin lace, and tie a knot as close as possible to one end. Thread the pony beads onto the lace, and tie a knot in the other end. Hand-stitch the lace flat to each side of the pouch, onto the space at each side of the embroidery, leaving 3.2cm (1¼in) of lace hanging down each side with the beads on.

Round coin purse

By taking the quarter rosette motifs from each corner of the chart, and stitching them together to make a circle, you can create this authentic-looking purse.

✿ White Aida fabric, 18-count, 10.5cm (4¼in) square
✿ Contrasting backing fabric, 10.5cm (4¼in) square
✿ Medium weight iron-on interfacing, 10.5cm (4¼in) square
✿ DMC stranded cotton (floss) in the colours listed on the chart
✿ Tapestry needle No 26
✿ 10cm (4in) zip fastener
✿ Matching sewing thread
✿ One deerskin lace, 63.5cm (25in) long
✿ Six pony beads in colours to complement the embroidery

1 Prepare your fabric, find the starting point (see page 10) then, following the corner motifs from the chart on pages 82–85, work the design as a complete circle. You may wish to photocopy and stick together the pieces to make a complete chart before you start. Use two strands of stranded cotton (floss) throughout.

2 Press the finished embroidery face down (see page 12). Then, iron the interfacing on to the wrong side.

3 Cut the Aida to shape, leaving 13mm (½in) of unworked fabric all round the embroidery. Cut the backing fabric to the same size.

4 Place the embroidery right side up on a flat surface with the backing fabric on top, right sides together. Pin, tack (baste), and mchine the zip in place at the top between the two pieces of fabric. Pin and tack (baste) a 13mm (½in) seam round the rest of the circle. Machine-stitch the tacked (basted) seams and then clip the curves of the excess fabric. Machine-stitch another row of stitching, 7mm (¼in) outside the first row, and trim the seam close to the stitching. Remove the pins and tacking (basting) stitches, and turn to the right side.

5 Take the deerskin lace, and tie a knot as close as possible to one end. Thread the pony beads onto the lace, and tie a knot in the other end. Hand-stitch 2.5cm (1in) of the lace to each side of the purse, just below the zip. Leave 7.5cm (3in) of lace with three beads threaded on the end hanging down each side.

Stitch parts of the Nez Perce Tribeswoman chart on page 82–85 to make these small gifts: a friendship bag pouch or a round coin purse.

DMC STRANDED
COTTON (FLOSS)

Symbol	Colour	Symbol	Colour
·	Blanc	●	823
T	300	▣	824
Z	301	∅	826
⊙	304	⌋	827
÷	307	◣	839
■	310	◥	840
▤	311	∨	842
✳	317	▥	891
↑	318	I	894
◆	321	↗	895
✕	350	▨	898
S	352	−	931
◼	355	►	934
F	356	▢	946
▣	413	∧	950
→	414	◺	963
△	422	✓	972
←	471	⊕	973
●	517	▜	975
▽	553	N	976
✕	610	⊠	986
I	640	◭	988
‖	676	H	995
◁	677	↓	996
↙	721	▦	9001
⋮	745	⁒	3047
⊍	781	◇	3064
○	783	4	3346
▣	796	+	3348
⚡	798	▲	3371
⌐	801	⋂	3607
◀	815	▤	3766

Nez Perce tribeswoman

DMC STRANDED COTTON (FLOSS)

Symbol	Code		Symbol	Code
⊡	Blanc		●	823
T	300		▣	824
Z	301		∅	826
◙	304		⅃	827
÷	307		◤	839
■	310		◩	840
▤	311		∨	842
✳	317		▥	891
↑	318		I	894
◈	321		↗	895
▨	350		▧	898
S	352		−	931
◨	355		►	934
F	356		▦	946
⊙	413		∧	950
→	414		↘	963
△	422		∫	972
←	471		⊹	973
◆	517		▜	975
∨	553		N	976
✕	610		⊠	986
I	640		◺	988
‖	676		H	995
<	677		↓	996
↳	721		◣	3031
∴	745		⅍	3047
U	781		◇	3064
O	783		4	3346
◙	796		+	3348
ϟ	798		▲	3371
⌐	801		⌂	3607
◤	815		=	3766

Navajo Weaving

According to a famous Navajo legend, 'Spider Woman instructed the Navajo women how to weave on a loom, which Spider Man told them how to make, with crosspoles of sky and earth cords, warp sticks of sun rays, and heddles (harnesses that guide the threads in the loom) of rock crystal and sheet lightning'. In fact, the women learnt to weave from their Pueblo neighbours and developed their own bold and colourful patterns which they used on clothing and rugs.
The Native Indian art of weaving is currently undergoing a revival. Now you can recreate some of these striking patterns for your own home by stitching a traditional Navajo rug based on a Classic Phase III Chief's Blanket from the Navajo, Ganado, Arizona, c.1890. The crosses in the centre represent Spider Woman.

The Navajo obtained churro sheep from Spanish colonists. With their long, coarse wool, these sheep were perfect for their needs: they reproduced easily, were resistant to disease, and their wool was ideal for hand-weaving. They made clothing from wool and from the cotton they planted, and traded woven goods with neighbouring tribes throughout the Southwest.

The rug

This eyecatching rug is worked in only three colours and finished off with a line of tassels at each end.

✡ Cream Aida fabric, 11-count, 44.3 x 35.5cm (17½ x 14in)
✡ Contrasting backing fabric, 44.3 x 35.5cm (17½ x 14in)
✡ Medium-weight iron-on interfacing, 44.3 x 35.5cm (17½ x 14in)
✡ DMC stranded cotton (floss) in the colours listed on the chart
✡ Tapestry needle No 24
✡ Matching sewing thread
✡ Twenty-eight black tassels (see page 14 for how to make a tassel)

1 Prepare your fabric, find the starting point (see page 10) then, following the Navajo Rug chart on pages 88 and 89, work the design downwards. Use three strands of stranded cotton (floss) throughout.

2 When you have completed the embroidery, place it face down on a soft cloth or towel and press it carefully (see page 12). Then, iron the interfacing on to the wrong side.

3 Place the embroidery right side up on a firm, flat surface with the backing fabric on top, right sides together. Pin and tack (baste) round three sides of the rug, leaving one short side open. Machine-stitch the tacked (basted) seams as close to the embroidery as you can, in a 13mm (½in) seam. Clip the excess fabric from the corners, remove the pins and tacking (basting) stitches, and turn to the right side.

4 Press in the seam allowance along the open edge, and slip stitch the edges together. Stitch 14 tassels to each short side by hand, with one at each corner, and the others evenly spaced, 2.5cm (1in) apart, in between.

Navajo belt

Use the central design from the Navajo Rug chart on page 88 and 89 as a repeating pattern, with the order of the thread colours reversed, to make an unusual belt. Deerskin laces, pony beads and feathers add authentic finishing touches.

✡ Red scalloped-edge Linen band, 7.5cm (3in) wide, 5cm (2in) longer than the required waist measurement
✡ Contrasting backing fabric, 9.5cm (3¾in) wide, 7.5cm (3in) shorter than the linen band
✡ Medium-weight iron-on interfacing 7cm (2¾in) wide, the length of the belt
✡ DMC stranded cotton (floss) in the colours listed on the chart
✡ Matching sewing thread

✤ Tapestry needle No 26
✤ Craft adhesive
✤ Six deerskin laces, 30.5cm (12in) long
✤ Eighteen pony beads in colours to complement the embroidery
✤ Twelve small feathers – I used Guinea Hen Fluffs (available from Pearce Tandy Leathercraft Ltd, see page 127)

1 Prepare your Linen band, find the centre point (see page 10), then following the chart on page 88–89, work the design from the centre out to each end, stitching the motifs in black with a red centre. Leave 4cm (1½in) of unworked fabric at each end. Use one strand of stranded cotton (floss) throughout.

2 When you have completed the embroidery, lay it face down on a soft cloth or towel and press it carefully (see page 12). Then, iron the interfacing on to the wrong side with the iron on a medium setting.

3 Take the backing fabric, and press under 10mm (⅜in) on both long edges. With right sides facing, pin the backing to the embroidered Linen band along each short side in a 13mm (½in) seam and stitch.

4 Turn to the right side, and pin the backing fabric to the linen band just below the scalloped edge. Slip stitch into place. The backing should be 2.5cm (1in) away from each end of the belt.

5 Position the deerskin laces along the wrong side of the belt so that they are evenly spaced, and lined up well with the design. Stitch them down by hand. Thread three pony beads onto the end of each lace, and attach two feathers to the ends. See page 14 for how to attach feathers to laces.

Make a rug and a belt based on a simple, yet striking Navajo pattern.

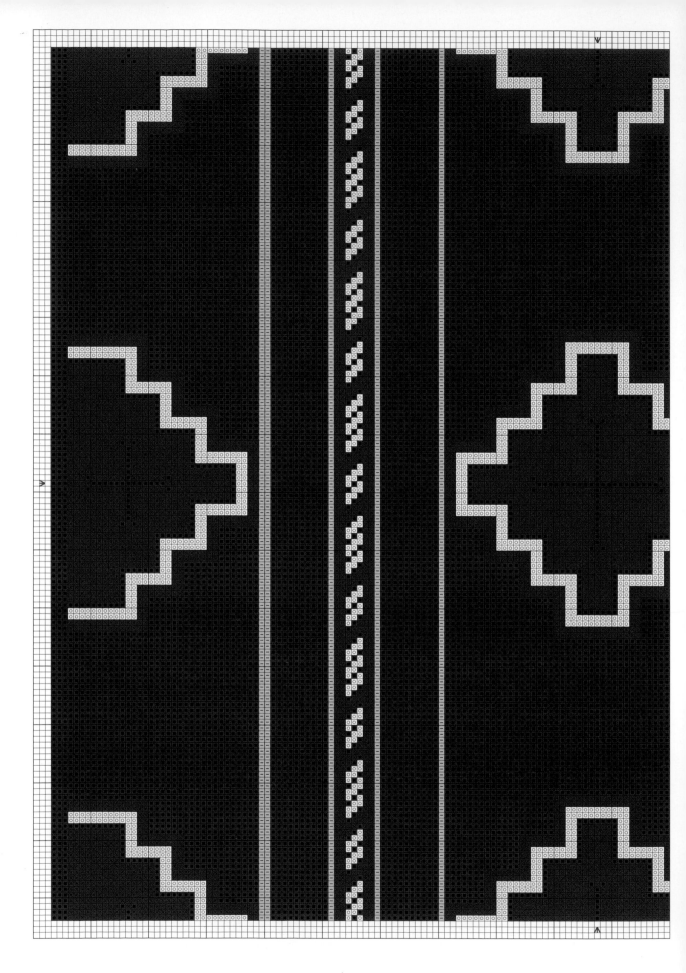

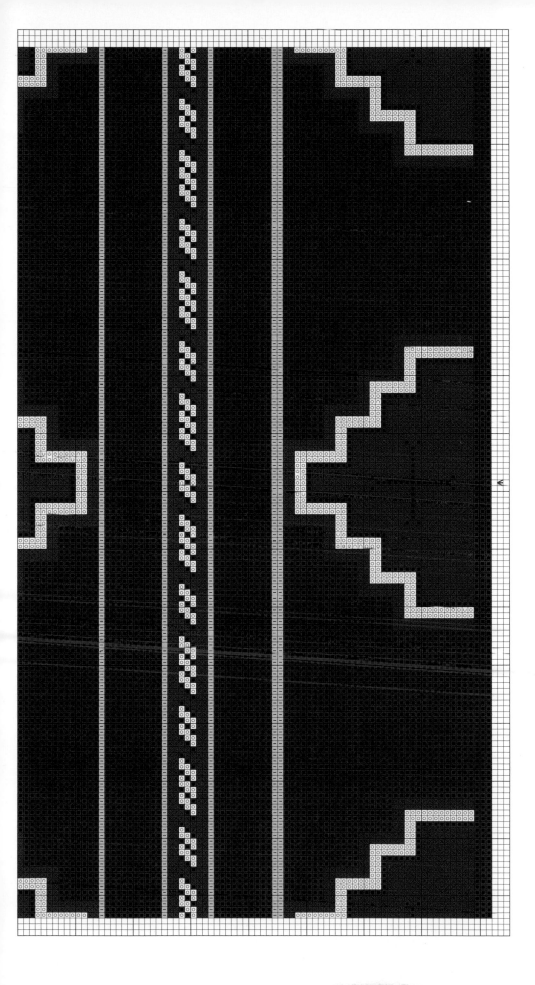

Navajo Rug

DMC STRANDED
COTTON (FLOSS)

- ■ 310
- ✕ 606
- – 676
- ⊙ 746

Pueblo Pottery

Throughout the states of New Mexico and Arizona, you will find the ancient towns and ruins of the Pueblo people. 'Pueblo' is a Spanish word for town, and refers to the Native American Indians who for centuries have lived in villages or cities in the South-west region.

The Pueblo people are a very advanced primitive society, who still practise their traditional skills of basket-making, weaving, pottery and building today. It was the beautiful, dramatic style of their pottery that gave me the inspiration for this design. It features a terracotta food bowl and some water vases, decorated with simple, yet highly effective, geometric motifs. I have added a border in the same style around the design.

The framed picture

You can either stitch the whole picture to go in a frame, or the vase alone to go in a greetings card.

- White Aida fabric, 14-count, 38 x 41cm (15 x 16¼in)
- DMC stranded cotton (floss) in the colours listed on the chart
- Tapestry needle, No 24
- Firm mounting board, 30.5 x 33.5cm (12 x 13¼in)
- Masking tape
- Picture frame of your choice

1 Prepare your fabric, find the starting point (see page 10) then, following the Pueblo Pottery chart on pages 92 and 93, work the design downwards. Use two strands of stranded cotton (floss) for the cross stitch, and one strand for the backstitch.

2 When you have completed the embroidery, place it face down on a soft cloth or towel and press it carefully (see page 12).

3 See 'Mounting embroideries for framing' on page 12 to mount and frame the finished embroidery.

Greetings card

Stitch one of the Pueblo vases to go on its own in a greetings card you have decorated with line drawings taken from the Pictographs on page 122.

- Sky blue Aida fabric, 18-count, 17.5cm x 14.5cm (7 x 5¾in)
- DMC stranded cotton (floss) in the colours listed on the chart
- Tapestry needle, No. 26
- Thin card in a colour of your choice, 45.5 x 26cm (18 x 10¼in)
- Contrasting thin card, 24 x 21cm (9½ x 8¼in)
- Double-sided adhesive tape
- Scalpel or craft knife
- Black indelible-ink art pen

1 Prepare your fabric, find the starting point (see page 10) then, following the large water vase section of the chart on pages 92–93, work the design downwards. Use two strands of stranded cotton (floss) throughout.

2 Place your completed embroidery face down on a soft cloth or towel and press carefully (see page 12). Iron the interfacing to the wrong side if using.

3 See page 46, point 3 for how to cut out your card: it should have an aperture of 15 x 13.5cm (6 x 5⅜in). See 'Transferring motifs on to card mounts' on page 14, and 'Mounting embroidery in a card' on page 13.

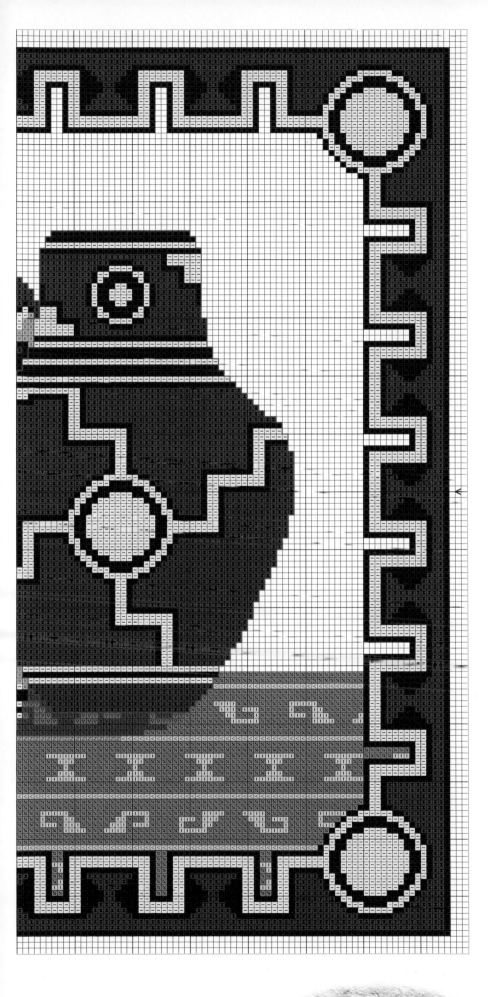

Pueblo Pottery

DMC STRANDED
COTTON (FLOSS)

▽	209
I	211
■	310
Z	813
−	822
<	827
■	918
✕	921
S	3041
✕	3042
II	3782

Backstitch
| ╱ | 414 |

Sand Painting

Sand painting was an important part of
Navajo religious life. It took place in a
healing or blessing ceremony known as a
'Chant' or 'Sing', which lasted for
anything from one to nine days.

Clean sand was spread over the floor for
the medicine-man and his assistants to
draw on with coloured powders ground
from minerals and charcoal. They would
skilfully sift the powders between their
thumb and finger to create pictures on
the sand. These images, and the chanting
that accompanied every ceremony, would
attract the Spirits.

The 'patient', for whom the ceremony was
being sung, would sit on the sand
painting facing east. The chanter then
took sand from the figures and applied
them to the patient to let the power of the
Spirits be transferred to them for healing
or blessing. When the ceremony was over
the sand painting would be carefully
erased and the sand cast to the wind.

The figures from the sand painting design can also be stitched
individually to make an exciting set of framed pictures. I used
beige 27-count Linda and worked the designs in one strand
over one thread of the fabric. I chose the same bright red
frame for each picture.

The throw
You can either stitch the whole chart on a large square
of Linda fabric to make a throw, or stitch the figures
on their own to go in frames.

✿ Beige Linda fabric, 27-count, 80.5 x 78.5cm (31¾ x 30⅞in)
✿ DMC stranded cotton (floss) in the colours listed on the chart
✿ Tapestry needle, No 26

1 Prepare your fabric, find the starting point (see page
10) then, following the Sand Painting charts on pages
96 to 99, work the design. You may wish to photocopy
and stick together the pieces to make a complete chart
before you start. Use two strands of stranded cotton
(floss) for the cross stitch, stitching over two fabric
threads, to make 14 stitches to the inch.

2 When you have completed the embroidery, place
it face down on a soft cloth or towel and press it carefully (see page 12).

3 Place the embroidery right side up on a firm, flat surface, and by carefully removing one fabric thread at
a time, fray all round the four raw edges for 2.5cm (1in).

The sand painting figures
This design is based on a sand painting from a Navajo
shooting chant, a complex and important healing
ceremony. The figures represent Black Thunder, Blue
Thunder, Water Ox and Water Horse.
The Thunders have wings instead of arms and a tail
like a bird, and are very elaborate. The tail carries
rain and the curves on the bottom represent the
reverberation of Thunder. The two Thunders are in
contrasting colours to show that each one has not
only his own power, but also that of his partner opposite. The white lines coming down from their wings
are lightning.
Water Ox is 'the adulterous child of Thunder'. He has
a similar body to the Thunders, except it is longer
and narrower. He has arms not wings, and horns with
soft feathers at the ends.
The Water Horse has four rainbows on its body, with
two more to make its horns, and lightning on its
forelegs, mane and tail, and coming out of its mouth.
The centre motif illustrates the home of the
Thunders. The symbolism shows a black mountain to
the east where Black Thunder sits, and a blue
mountain to the west where Blue Thunder sits.

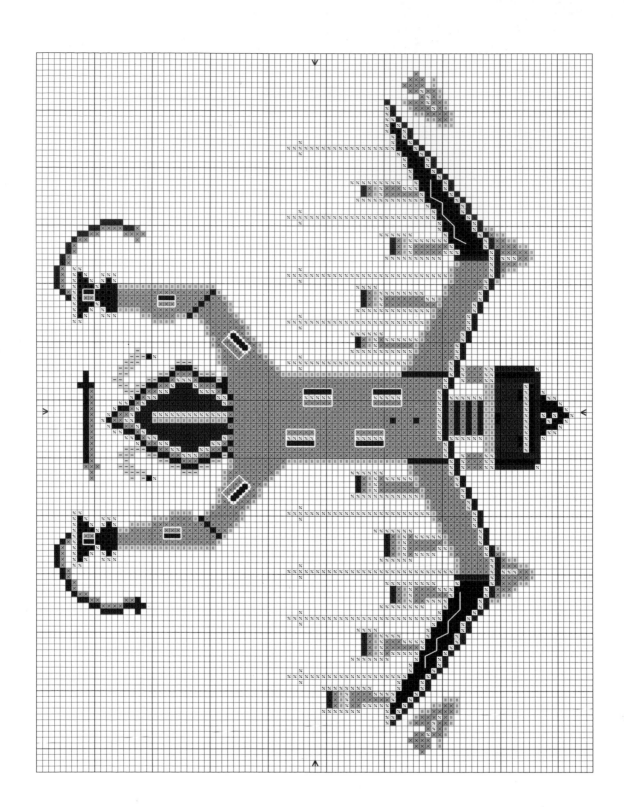

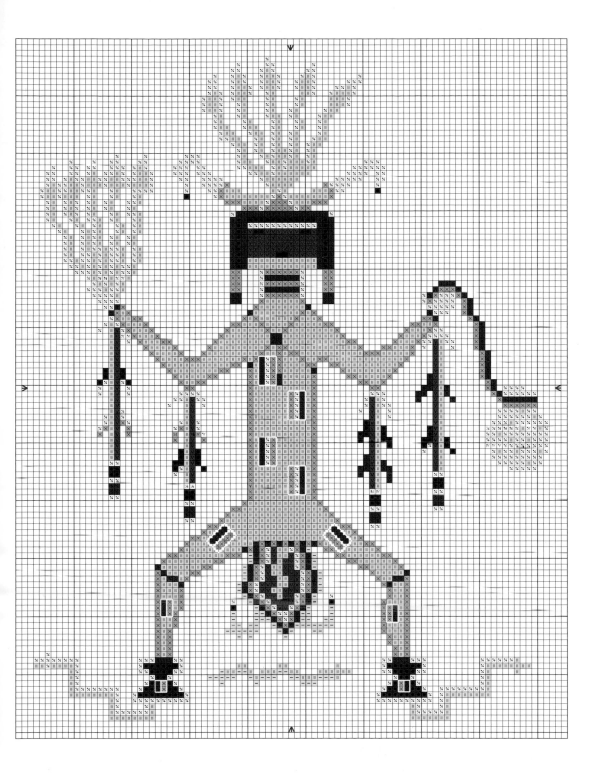

Sand painting throw

DMC Stranded Cotton (Floss)

☒	Blanc
■	310
⑤	349
⊟	818
☒	932
▼	975
‖	3822

Backstitch

◤	Blanc
◹	3822

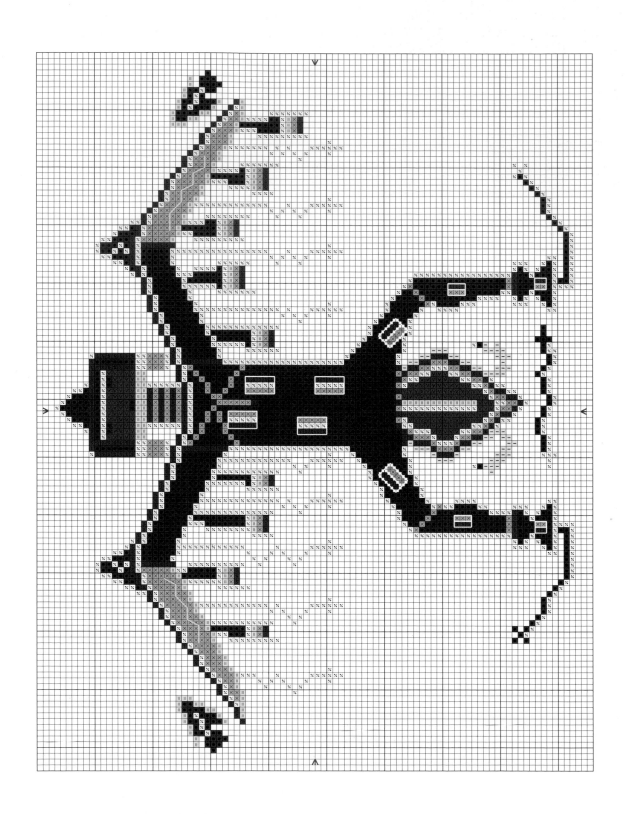

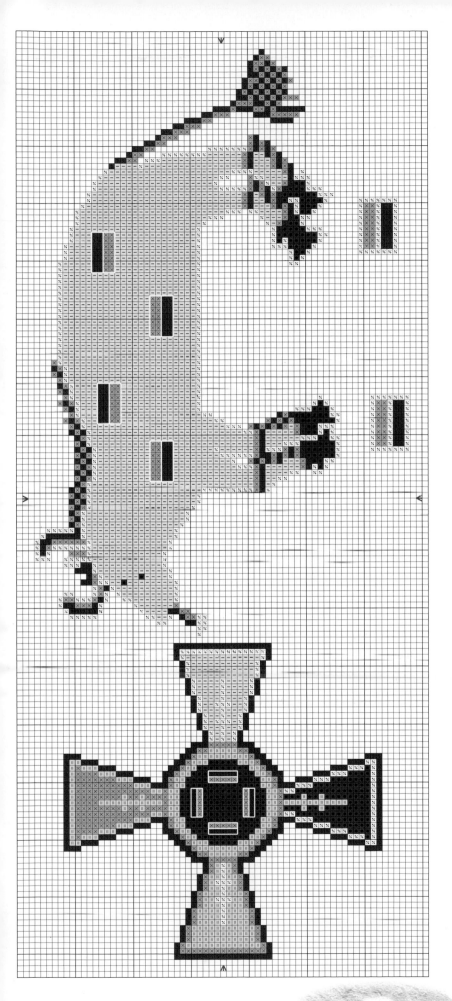

Sand painting throw

DMC Stranded Cotton (Floss)

- ⌘ Blanc
- ● 310
- ▨ 349
- − 818
- ⊠ 932
- ▼ 975
- ‖ 3822

Backstitch
- ◪ Blanc
- ◹ 3822

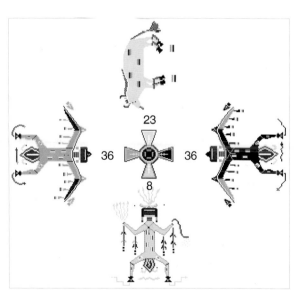

23

36   36

8

Use this diagram to help you position the elements of the Sand Painting throw on your fabric. Plan the overall design on graph paper before you start – the figures indicate the number of squares to leave between each motif. Stitch over two threads, using two strands of stranded cotton (floss) for the cross stitch.

Woodland Tribes Motifs

These cushion designs are based on the elaborate beadwork made by the Eastern Woodland tribes. The tribes decorated clothing and other items like their bandolier bags in this simple, yet effective, style. The geometric design is from the Potawatomi tribe, Kansas c.1890, and the floral design from the Great Lakes c.1890.

I have finished off the cushions in two different ways, both in keeping with the American Indian theme. One has embroidered tabs ending in small tassels, and the other has long beaded tassels. You can use either effect on both cushions, so the choice is yours. I also used the motifs to decorate a shirt front and a pin cushion.

To make a cushion pad

If you cannot find cushion pads of the desired size in the shops, follow these three easy steps to make your own.

1. Add an extra 2.5cm (1in) to the stated cushion pad dimensions, for a seam allowance, and cut two pieces of calico or similar fabric to size.

2. Pin the pieces together, right sides facing, and stitch all round, leaving an opening of about 10cm (4in) at one side. Clip excess fabric from the corners and turn to the right side.

3. Stuff firmly with kapok, then turn in the raw edges of the opening and slip stitch together.

The cushions

Follow the materials listing and the instructions below to make the two cushions and trim them with either tabs or tassels. See page 14 for how to make your own tassels. Cushion fabric measurements include a 13mm (½in) seam allowance, and tab fabric measurements include a 10mm (⅜in) seam allowance.

For the geometric cushion you will need:

✡ White Aida fabric, 14-count, 23.5 x 33cm (9¼x 13in)
✡ Contrasting backing fabric, 23.5 x 33cm (9¼ x 13in)
✡ DMC stranded cotton (floss) in the colours listed on the chart
✡ Tapestry needle, No 24
✡ 34 tassels in colours to match the stranded cotton (floss)
✡ 68 black pony beads
✡ Matching sewing thread
✡ Cushion pad, 20.5 x 30cm (8 x 11¾in)

For the floral cushion you will need:

✡ Colonial blue Aida, 14-count, 31.5 x 25.5cm (12½ x 10in)
✡ Colonial blue Aida, 14-count, 22 strips measuring 7.5 x 16.5cm (3 x 6⅝in) each for the tabs
✡ Contrasting backing fabric, 31.5 x 25.5cm (12½ x 10in)
✡ DMC stranded cotton (floss) in the colours listed on the chart
✡ Tapestry needle, No 24
✡ Twenty-two tassels in colours to match the stranded cotton (floss)
✡ Sewing thread to match the fabric
✡ Cushion pad, 30.5 x 24cm (12 x 9½in)

To make the cushion:

1 Prepare your fabric, find the starting point (see page 10) then, following the geometric chart on pages 106–107 or the floral chart on pages 104–105, work the design downwards. Use two strands of cotton (floss).

2 When you have completed the embroidery, place it face down on a soft cloth or towel and press it carefully (see page 12).

3 Place your embroidery right side up on a firm, flat surface (if adding tabs, arrange them evenly along both long edges, with all raw edges level, and the embroidered sides on the tabs and the cushion facing. Pin and tack (baste) in place).

4 Place the backing over the embroidery, right sides together. Pin and tack (baste) round three sides.

5 Machine-stitch the tacked (basted) seams and clip excess fabric from the corners. Remove the pins and tacking (basting) stitches, and turn to the right side.

6 Press in the seam allowance along each side of the opening. Place the cushion pad inside the cover, and oversew the edges together.

7 If you are making a cushion with tabs, stitch a tassel to the point of each tab. Alternatively, thread two pony beads on to each tassel, and hand-stitch 17 tassels down each long edge of the cushion, ensuring that they are evenly spaced.

To make the embroidered tabs:

1 Prepare your fabric (see page 10) and find your starting point, in the centre 1cm (⅜in) down from the top edge. Then, following design number 12 from the Pattern Library on page 114, stitch the pattern downwards. Use two strands of stranded cotton (floss) for the cross stitch.

2 When you have embroidered all 22 tabs, place them face down on a soft cloth or towel and press carefully (see page 12).

3 With right sides facing, fold each tab in half lengthways and stitch the seam. Press the seam open with the embroidery central, and stitch to a point at the bottom of each tab, 13mm (½in) below the embroidery. Clip the excess fabric from the point, turn the tab to the right side and press.

Potawatomi pin cushion

Use one of the central motifs from the geometric chart on pages 106–107 to create a third design, which can be made into a pretty pin cushion.

✡ Sky blue Aida fabric, 18-count, 12.6cm (5in) square
✡ Contrasting backing fabric, 12.6cm (5in) square
✡ DMC stranded cotton (floss) in the colours listed on the chart
✡ Tapestry needle, No 26
✡ Four tassels in a colour to match the stranded cotton (floss)
✡ Four black pony beads
✡ Matching sewing thread
✡ Small amount of kapok or polyester filling
Measurements include a 13mm (½in) seam allowance

1 Follow steps 1–5 (left) for making a cushion. Press in the seam allowance on the open edge, and stuff the pin cushion firmly with kapok or polyester filling. Slip stitch the seam together, adding more filling as you go.

2 Thread a pony bead onto each tassel if desired, and hand-stitch a tassel to each corner.

Embroidered shirt

Make a plain shirt look really special by embroidering it with the repeating leaf design from the floral cushion chart on pages 104–105, using waste canvas.

✧ Plain cotton shirt
✧ Waste canvas, 14-count, two 45.5 x 10.5cm (18 x 4¼in) pieces
✧ DMC stranded cotton (floss) in colours listed on chart
✧ Tacking (basting) thread
✧ Sharp or crewel needle
✧ Pair of fine tweezers
✧ Spray-bottle of water

1 For each motif, cut a piece of waste canvas about 4cm (1½in) wider and deeper than the finished design will be.

2 Align the coloured threads in the waste canvas with the weave of the shirt, or, align the waste canvas with a seam of the garment. Pin, then tack (baste) the waste canvas into position on each side of the shirt opening.

3 Stitch the repeating leaf design from the Floral Cushion chart on pages 104–105 following the waste canvas instructions for the Ceremonial Buffalo Skull project on page 42. Use two strands of stranded cotton (floss) for the cross stitch.

Here are two of the many different ways you can use these versatile Woodland Tribes motifs: Stitch the geometric design on blue aida and make a beautiful tasselled pin cushion, or liven up a shirt by embroidering the floral motifs down its front.

Woodland Tribes Cushions

DMC Stranded
Cotton (Floss)

⊠	726
▬	742
▪	823
▥	3328
◙	3346

Woodland Tribes Cushions

DMC STRANDED
COTTON (FLOSS)

- ⬛ 310
- ➕ 606
- ⊠ 726
- ➖ 742
- ⬛ 823
- Ⓤ 3326
- ◉ 3346
- ⊠ 3752
- ▲ 3755

Nez Perce Beading

The inspiration for this shoulder bag design came from a beaded bag attributed to the Nez Perce tribe. The original is beaded in the Transmontaine style popular on the Plateau and with the Crow tribe. Typical of this style are complex angular designs, a wide range of bead colours and pastel backgrounds. The other side would be beaded in a different design, but I backed my design with fabric in a contrasting colour.

Nez Perce bag

For an authentic finish, I trimmed my bag with 23 white fluffy feathers hanging from deerskin laces, and a deerskin lace hanging strap.

✡ White Aida fabric, 18-count, 14 x 21cm (5½ x 8¼in)
✡ Contrasting backing fabric, 14 x 21cm (5½ x 8¼in)
✡ Lining fabric, two 14 x 21cm (5½ x 8¼in) pieces
✡ DMC stranded cotton (floss) in the colours listed on the chart
✡ Matching sewing thread
✡ Tapestry needle No 26
✡ One deerskin lace, 137cm (54in) long
✡ Twenty-three deerskin laces, 12.5cm (5in) long
✡ Twenty-five 3cm (1⅛in) metal cones
✡ Twenty-three White Fluffy Plumes
✡ Six metal charms or feathers to hang from the laces on the bag strap. I used four 5cm (2in) silver-plated stamped metal feathers, and two silver-plated coyote charms.
✡ Scalpel or craft knife
✡ Craft adhesive

1 Prepare your fabric, find the starting point (see page 10) then, following the Nez Perce bag chart on page 110, work the design downwards. Use two strands of stranded cotton (floss) throughout.

2 Place your completed embroidery face down on a soft cloth or towel and press carefully (see page 12).

3 Thread a metal cone onto each of the 23 deerskin laces, and fix a White Fluffy Plume to the end of each one (see page 14).

4 Place the embroidery right side up on a firm, flat surface, and apply craft adhesive to the undecorated end of each lace on the right side. Fix the laces side by side to the unstitched fabric of the seam allowance on one short edge, laying the laces and feathers with the right sides facing the right side of the embroidery.

5 Place the backing fabric on top, right sides facing, with the feathers and laces sandwiched in between. Pin and tack (baste) a 13mm (½in) seam along three edges, leaving the top open. Machine stitch these edges. Take care not to catch the feathers in the stitching.

6 Clip any excess fabric from the corners, remove the pins and tacking (basting) and turn to the right side. The feathered laces should hang at the bottom.

7 Put the two lining pieces together with right sides facing, and pin and tack (baste) along the long edges. Machine stitch a 13mm (½in) seam, leaving both short ends open. DO NOT TURN.

8 With right sides together and the side seams in line, slip the embroidered work inside the lining. Stitch the lining to the bag, around the top edge, in a 13mm (½in) seam. Turn to the right side through the opening in the bottom of the lining. Press in the seam allowance on the opening, and sew up. Push the lining into the bag.

9 Thread the metal cones on to the long deerskin lace. Using the scalpel, split the end of each lace into three 7.5cm (3in) strands. Thread your metal accessories (or feathers), on to the six lace strands, and fix into place with a little craft adhesive as described on page 14. Bring a metal cone down to each decorated end.

10 Starting at the top, hand-stitch 5cm (2in) of the lace to each side seam of the bag. Leave a 15cm (6in) decorated end hanging down each side.

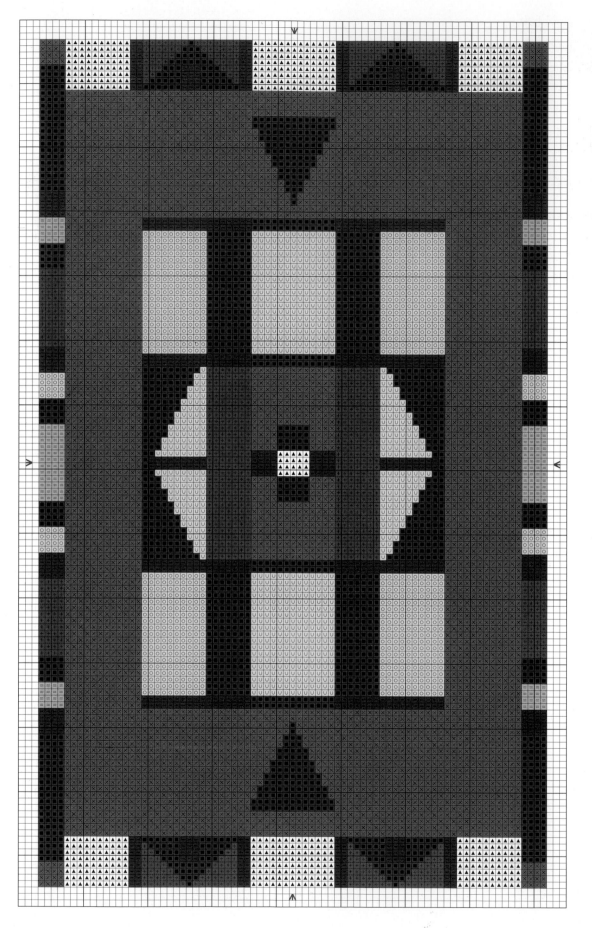

Nez Perce bag
DMC Stranded
Cotton (Floss)

▲	Blanc
▤	318
✕	553
✚	561
▬	666
■	797
U	827
⊙	973

Pattern Library

This section contains 32 patterns, symbols and motifs from different eras of Native American Indian life, with many shown stitched. Refer to the captions for the threads and fabrics used.

Make your own jewellery

Many tribes created their own distinctive geometric patterns to decorate clothing and other items. You can recreate the same style using modern embroidery materials and techniques to great effect. The bear tracks, tipi, man and woman, rain clouds and sun charted on page 116 are all shown here stitched on a waistcoat using 14-count waste canvas as a grid for the stitches. Directions on stitching with waste canvas can be found on page 42. You can also make your own Native American-style jewellery. The Pueblo thunderbird and the man and woman also charted on page 116, and the buffalo from page 117 are shown here stitched on 14-count perforated paper using two strands of stranded cotton (floss), and mounted on jewellery findings available from most craft shops. I used 5.5cm (2¼in) French hair barrettes to make the hair slides and 2cm (¾in) pinbacks for the brooches. I outlined each motif with relief outliner (see page 10) and backed it with iron-on interfacing before fixing it to the jewellery finding with craft adhesive.

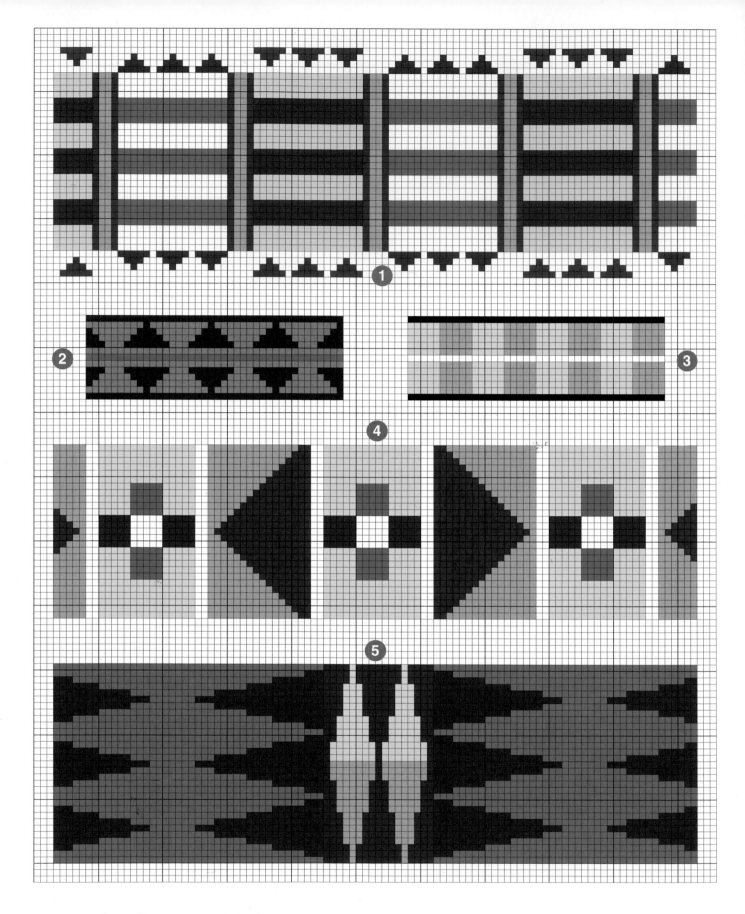

1 Beaded design from a Cheyenne woman's leggings
2 & 3 Designs from Nez Perce cornhusk bags
4 Beaded design from a Crow horse collar
5 Hidatsa porcupine quill design from a man's shirt, dated 1910

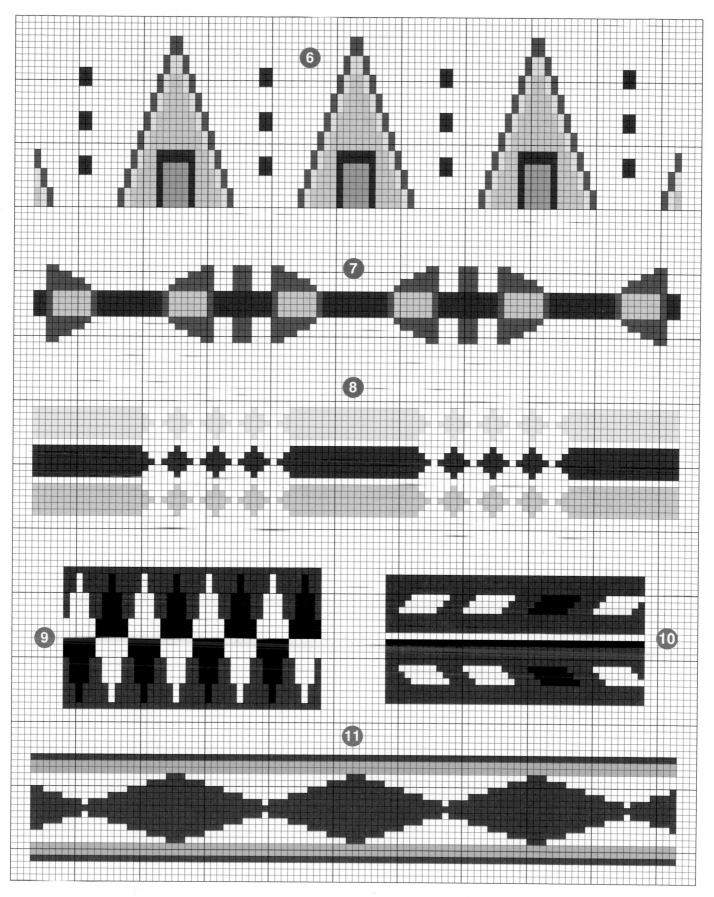

6 Beaded design from a Crow woman's leggings

7 Beaded design from Cheyenne one-piece leggings and moccasins, dated 1891

8 Beaded design from an Osage breechclout

9 Navajo design from a woollen saddle throw, dated 1886

10 Navajo design from a woollen blanket, dated 1893

11 Tewa Pueblo Indian design from a belt worn with a manta from the Santa Clara corn dance costume, dated 1950

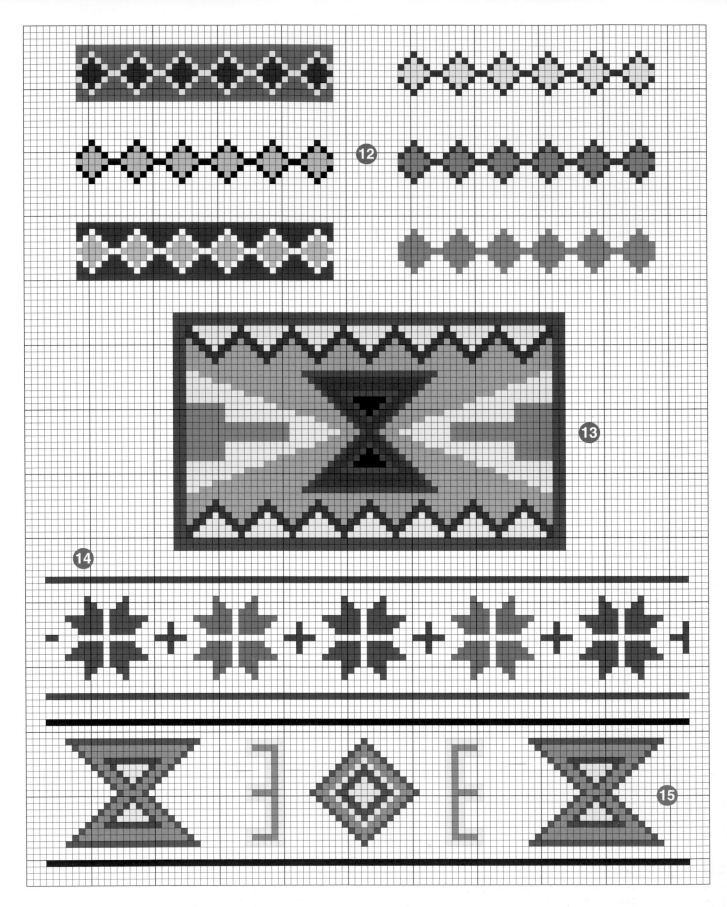

12 Beaded designs from a Potawatomi bandolier shoulder bag, dated 1890

13 Design from a painted rawhide parfleche or pouch from the Plains Indians

14 & 15 Beaded designs from legging strips from the Woodland tribes

Clever gift ideas

Mounted in a money box, the Hopi Kokopelli flute player charted on page 117 would make an ideal gift for a child or an adult friend to put their loose change in. It is stitched on 27-count light blue Linda fabric in two strands of stranded cotton (floss). The design is mounted in the box behind a removable plexiglas sheet. It's a good idea to wipe the plexiglas with a lint-free cloth before sliding it back into the box. Many of the designs in this section are the ideal size for decorating the lid of a trinket pot. The deer, symbol for warding off evil spirits and raindrop charted on page 117 are shown here displayed in different sized trinket pots, and the buffalo tracks from the same page in a scissors case. They have all been stitched on 22-count Hardanger fabric using one strand of stranded cotton (floss) and mounted in Framecraft products.

16 Pueblo thunderbird design: the thunderbird is the sacred
   bearer of happiness
17 Bear tracks
18 Tipi – temporary home

19 Mountains
20 Man and woman
21 Rain clouds – symbol of good prospects
22 Sun

23 Hopi Kokopelli flute player believed to bring abundance and fertility
24 Deer
25 Horse – symbol for a journey
26 Bird – representing the Sky Father, the energy and strength of
   the heavens. It symbolises detachment from the things of the
   earth – freedom, loftiness, idealism and fortitude.
27 Gila Monster – a sign of the desert

28 Symbol for warding off evil spirits
29 Buffalo tracks
30 Raindrop – symbol for plentiful crops
31 Cactus – another sign of the desert
32 The Buffalo was an Elder, a teacher of men. It symbolises
   the leader, and is an image of long life, representing provision,
   abundance and power.

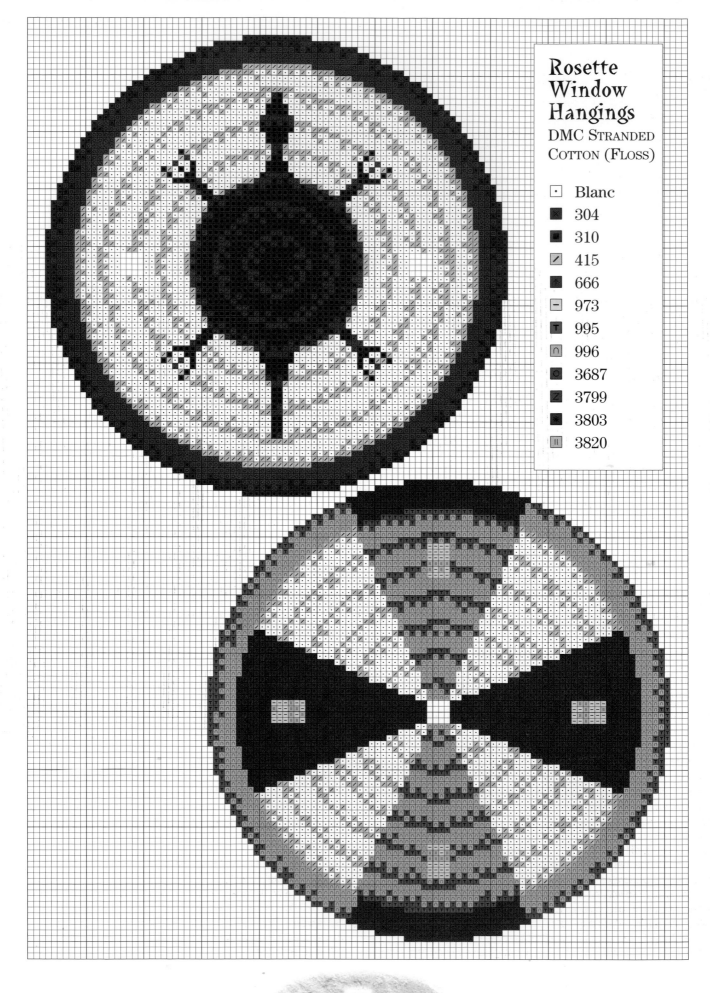

Rosette
Window
Hangings
DMC STRANDED
COTTON (FLOSS)

·	Blanc
✕	304
■	310
⁄	415
■	666
−	973
T	995
∩	996
◉	3687
◪	3799
✳	3803
‖	3820

Rosette window hangings

Native American Indian women would make beautiful rosettes to embellish shirt fronts, head-dresses, moccasins, cradleboard covers, quivers and pouches. They were first made from porcupine quills and later in beadwork. Rosettes provide the perfect inspiration for the two final window hangings in the book. Like the Sun Catcher and the Medicine Wheel on page 29, they are stitched on perforated paper and decorated with jewels, beads, feathers and charms.

Each window hanging is stitched on a 23 x 30.5cm (9 x 12in) sheet of ecru perforated paper using two strands of stranded cotton (floss) and backed with heavy-weight iron-on interfacing. Outline the design with black relief outliner and cut round it with a scalpel or craft knife (see points 1–4 on page 30).

The Turtle Rosette was finished off with two equal lengths of deerskin lace threaded with beads and feathers (see page 14), and

two 5/8in enamelled spot conchos. You will notice there are two unstitched areas on this chart, on either side of the turtle motif. Glue the tips of the decorated deerskin laces over these areas using craft adhesive. Then place the conchos on top and gently, but firmly, push the back prongs through the work without distorting it. Turn the embroidery over and bend back the prongs using thin pliers to fix the conchos in place.

The Morning Star window hanging is finished off with two long and two short deerskin laces threaded with pony beads, tin cones and stamped metal feathers (see page 14), and a 2.5cm (1in) Western Concho. Glue the tips of the deerskin laces to the unstitched area on the design using craft adhesive. Then take your concho and thread the laces through the vertical slits in the centre before gluing it in place with craft adhesive.

Other Ideas

Native American designs lend themselves to a variety of different cross stitch projects – too many, in fact, to include in the one book. In this chapter you'll find more of my suggestions for ways to stitch the charts. I hope they will inspire you to think up many more good ideas of your own.

Artefacts wristband

Make a wristband using the border from the Native American Artefacts design on page 46.

1 Cut a piece of 5cm (2in) wide scalloped-edge Aida band to fit round your wrist, with a 2.5cm (1in) seam allowance. Find the centre (see page 10), then following the border from the chart on pages 48–51, work the design out from the centre to each end, leaving 13mm (½in) unstitched at each end for seams. Use two strands of stranded cotton (floss) for the cross stitch, and one strand for the backstitch.

2 Press the finished embroidery (see page 12), then iron some medium-weight interfacing to the wrong side. Place your work right side up and stitch three deerskin laces on top with right sides together and lined up with the bead design on the embroidery.

3 Cut a piece of contrasting backing fabric and turn under 11mm (⅜in) on each long edge. Place this on top of the embroidery, right sides together, and stitch the short ends together in a 13mm (½in) seam, with the deerskin laces between the backing and the embroidery.

4 Turn to the right side, and pin and tack (baste) the backing in place. Slip stitch to the Aida band, remove the pins and tacking (basting) stitches.

Nez Perce choker

Make a choker using the decorative border from the portrait of the Nez Perce tribeswoman on page 80.

1 Cut a 34.5cm (13¾in) piece of 2.5cm (1in) scalloped-edged Aida band and find the centre (see page 12). Following the border design on the right of the chart on pages 82 to 85, work the design out from the centre to each end, leaving 4cm (1½in) unstitched at each end. Use two strands of stranded cotton (floss).

2 Press the finished embroidery (see page 12) and iron some medium-weight iron-on interfacing to the wrong side. Place the embroidery right side up on a flat surface and put four deerskin laces on top, level with the top and bottom of the embroidery, and sew on by hand.

3 Cut some backing fabric, and press under 1cm (⅜in) on each long edge. Place this over the embroidery, right sides together, and sew the short ends together in a 5mm (¼in) seam, with the deerskin laces in between.

4 Turn to the right side, and pin and tack (baste) the backing in place. Slip stitch to the Aida band, remove the pins and tacking (basting) stitches. Thread four pony beads on to the end of each lace, and attach a pressed metal feather to the end of each lace. See page 14 for how to attach feathers to laces.

Plains warrior placemat

Make a placemat using the border from the Plains warrior chart on pages 38–39. For each placemat you will need 37 x 30cm (14⅝x 11⅞in) of sky blue Aida.

1 Work the design in two strands of stranded cotton (floss) throughout. Press your completed embroidery (see page 12), then place your work on a firm, flat surface, and by carefully removing one fabric thread at a time, fray all round the four raw edges for 2.5cm (1in).

You don't have to stitch the whole chart – take individual motifs and borders from larger projects to work as smaller items. From top (clockwise) the War Club from page 48 is stitched over two on 27-count Linda to go in a frame, a Ceremonial Dance bookmark (see page 25 for directions), the Plains Warrior placemat, the Artefacts wristband, and the Nez Perce choker.

Pictographs

Use these Native American line drawings to decorate greetings cards or other items of your choice. See page 14 for how to transfer the motifs onto card mounts.

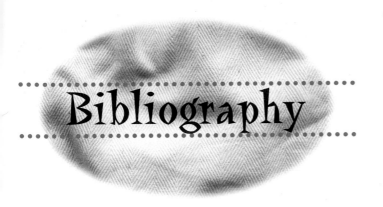

Bibliography

Anson Warner, John, T*he Life & Art of the North American Indian* (The Hamlyn Publishing Group Ltd., 1975)

Appleton, Le Roy H., *American Indian Design & Decoration* (Dover Publications Inc., 1971)

Burland, Cottie, *North American Indian Mythology* (Chancellor Press, 1996)

Davis, Christopher, *North American Indian* (The Hamlyn Publishing Group, 1969)

Dockstader, Frederick J., *Weaving Arts of the North American Indian* (Harper Collins Publishers Inc., 1993)

Edmonds, Susan, *Native Peoples of North America* (Cambridge University Press, 1993)

Feest, Christian F., *Native Arts of North America* (Thames & Hudson Ltd., 1992)

Griffin-Pierce, Trudy, *The Encyclopedia of Native America* (Rushfield Books, 1995)

Hagan, William T., *American Indians* (The University of Chicago Press Ltd., 1993)

Hunt, W. Ben, *The Complete How-to Book of Indiancraft* (Macmillan Publishing Company, 1973)

Johnson, Michael, *American Indians of the Southeast* (Reed International Books Ltd., 1995)

Jonaitis, Aldona, *From the Land of the Totem Poles* (British Museum Publications, 1988)

Mails, Thomas E., *The Mystic Warriors of The Plains* (Council Oak Books, 1991)

Murdoch, David, *North American Indian* (Dorling Kindersley Ltd., 1995)

Naylor, Maria, *Authentic Indian Designs* (Dover Publications Inc., 1975)

Paterek, Josephine, *Encyclopedia of American Indian Costume* (ABC-CLIO Inc., 1994)

Reichard, Gladys A., *Sandpaintings of the Navajo Shooting Chant* (Dover Publications Inc., 1975)

Schiffer, Nancy N., *Navajo Arts and Crafts* (Schiffer Publishing Ltd., 1991)

Sherman Josepha, *Indian Tribes of North America* (Todtri Productions Ltd., 1996)

Sherman Josepha, *The First Americans* (Tiger Books Int. Plc., 1996)

Smith Sides, Dorothy, *Decorative Art of The Southwestern Indians* (Dover Publications Inc., 1961)

Taylor, Colin F., Native *American Arts And Crafts* (Salamander Books Ltd, 1995)

Thom, Laine, *Becoming Brave* (Chronicle Books 1992)

Thom, Laine/ Brafford, C. J., *Dancing Colours* (Chronicle Books 1992)

Turner, Geoffrey, *Indians of North America* (Stirling Publishing Co. Inc., 1992)

Versluis, Arthur, *Native American Traditions* (Element Books Ltd., 1994)

Waldman, Carl, *Atlas of the North American Indian* (Facts On File Publications, 1985)

Walters, Anna Lee, *The Spirit of Native America* (Chronicle Books, 1989)

Wilson, Eva, *North American Indian Designs* (British Museum Press, 1995)

Wissler, Clark, *Indians of the United States* (Anchor Books, 1989)

Yenne, Bill, *The Encyclopedia Of North American Indian Tribes* (Magna Books, 1995)

Sacred Symbols Native Americans (Thames & Hudson Ltd., 1996)

The Native Americans (Tiger Books Int. Plc., 1995)

Useful Addresses

Survival International, 11–15 Emerald Street, London, WC1N 3QL
Survival International is a worldwide organisation supporting tribal peoples. It upholds their rights to decide their own future and helps them to protect their lives, lands and human rights. It stocks a wide range of publications on tribal peoples including Native Americans, and has a sales catalogue stocking many Native American-inspired art and craft goods.

Department of Anthropology, National Museum of Natural History, Smithsonian Institute, Washington DC, USA

The Forge North American Indian Museum, Forge Cottage, Station Road, Horsted Keynes, West Sussex, RH17 7AT
A collection of authentic artefacts, mostly from the Plains area, which shows the ingenuity, artistry and diversity of Native American art. Items date from approximately 1850 to the 1900s. Viewing by appointment only through Ian West (tel: 01825 790314).

The American Museum in Britain, Claverton Manor, Bath, BA2 7BD, Tel: (01225) 460503, Fax: (01225) 480726
Holds a collection of authentic artefacts from both the nineteenth- and twentieth-centuries, including Navajo jewellery, Plains Indian costumes, Eastern Woodlands embroidered pouches and much more, plus an extensive library of books on North American subjects. An annual Native American weekend is held in June, with displays of traditional North American Indian dances and songs.

Native American and Grey Owl Galleries, Hastings Museum and Art Gallery, Cambridge Road, Hastings, East Sussex, Tel: (01424) 781155
Has three galleries of Native American material, mainly from the Plains region. Special features include: figures of Blackfoot, Sioux and Aleutian Indians, a miniature Indian village, the inside of a tipi, and a wealth of artefacts including tomahawks, scalps, pipes, head-dresses, dance rattles and drums.

National Museum of Scotland, Chambers Street, Edinburgh, Scotland, EH1 1JF, Tel: (0131) 225 7534; Fax: (0131) 220 4819
Holds a substantial collection of decorated American Indian objects, the majority dating from the late-nineteenth and early-twentieth centuries. This includes quillwork, painted wood, pottery and embroidery.

University of Cambridge Museum of Archaeology and Anthropology, Downing Street, Cambridge, CB2 3DZ, Tel: (01223) 333516; Fax: (01223) 333517
The museum has extensive collections of North American artefacts. There are three cases of North American material on display in the permanent gallery of world anthropology, and North American material is also included in the archaeological gallery.

The Horniman Museum, 100 London Road, Forest Hill, London, SE23 3PQ, Tel: 0181-699 1872
Has the third-largest collection of North American artefacts in England, with a gallery containing examples of beadwork costumes, a seventeenth-century leather coat, as well as a South American section and a Northwest Coast section.

It also has a library containing over 20,000 books, 100 journal titles and audio-visual material on ethnography, natural history, and musical instruments. Materials are selected to help people understand the objects in the museum, to enable greater understanding of other cultures and the natural world we inhabit.

John Judkyn Memorial, Freshford Manor, Bath, BA3 6BX, Tel: (01225) 723312; Fax: (01225) 723730
Circulates small school exhibits on American themes, including a number relating to Native American Indians, for classroom use. They are available on loan to schools for teaching purposes and consist of easily transportable perspex-fronted cases containing a group of objects selected for the way in which they reflect a certain theme. Notes and graphic material are also provided.

Also puts together larger exhibitions, such as *The First Americans* and *Native American Portraits*, which are shown in museums and galleries throughout Britain and abroad.

Acknowledgements

I would like to give my thanks to the following people for their skilful sewing of the cross stitch embroideries featured in this book. I certainly couldn't have done the book without you all: Diana Hewitt, Maureen Hipgrave, Lynda Potter, Jenny Whitlock, Judy Riggans, Andrea Martin, Rita Boulton, Pat Chapman, Paloma Allen, Linda Guy, Lesley Buckerfield, Stella Baddeley, Patricia Ward, Louise Wells, Sue Clarke, Gillian Saunders and Angela Taylor. And for the making up of the projects, and practical advice for the instructions, Connie Woolcott. Thank you ladies for your lovely work and your loyalty over the years. It is much appreciated.

Large portraits of Chief Red Cloud, Sioux Warrior and Nez Perce Tribeswoman from original paintings by Leannda Cross, and Plains Warrior, End of The Trail and Coyote designs from original paintings by Collette Hoefkens. Thanks ladies, they make the book look beautiful!

Many thanks also to Tom Aird for the perfect mounting of the embroideries, and excellent framing service over the last 14 years.

I would also like to thank the following companies who have contributed embroidery threads, fabrics and accessories, for use in this book: Framecraft Miniatures Ltd., and DMC Creative World Ltd.

Charted designs reproduced in conjunction with Crafted Software.

Authentic Native American Indian artefacts used for photography props bought from: Rodeo & Rider, 71 Windmill Road, Luton, Bedfordshire, LU1 3XL.

Suppliers

Framecraft Miniatures Ltd, manufacture an extensive range of small frames, miniature boxes, jewellery, Crafta Cards and many other products that hold small cross stitch designs, and make exquisite gifts. Also suppliers of Mill Hill beads and perforated needlework paper.

Framecraft items and accessories are available from:
- ✿ Framecraft Miniatures Ltd, 372–376 Summer Lane, Hockley, Birmingham B19 3QA.
- ✿ Gay Bowles Sales Inc, PO Box 1060, Janesville, WI, USA
- ✿ Ireland Needlecraft Pty Ltd, 2–4 Keppel Drive, Hallam, Victoria 3803, Australia
- ✿ Anne Brinkley Designs Inc, 761 Palmer Avenue, Holmdel, NJ 97733, USA
- ✿ The Embroidery Shop, Greville-Parker, 286 Queen Street, Masterton, New Zealand

Stranded embroidery cottons, Zweigart evenweave fabrics and other DMC products featured in this book are available from:

- ✿ DMC Creative World Ltd, Pullman Road, Wigston, Leicester LE8 2DY.
- ✿ DMC Needlecraft Pty, PO Box 317, Earlswood 2206, New South Wales 2204, Australia
- ✿ The DMC Corporation, Port Kearney Bld, #10 South Kearney, NJ 070732-0650, USA

Pony beads, conchos, Lobo Bolo slides, jewellery findings, Critter Spots, feathers and fluffs, dance bells, charms, deerskin laces, bone hair pipes, metal cones, stamped-metal feathers and many other American Indian craft accessories are available from Pearce Tandy Leathercraft Ltd.

- ✿ Billing Park, Northampton, NN3 9BG, UK, Tel: (01604) 407177
- ✿ 140 East Exchange Avenue, Fort Worth, USA

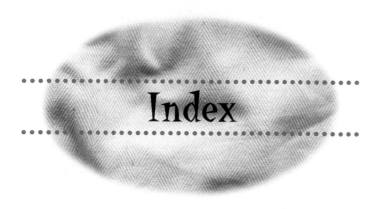

Index